Internet
Dates
From Hell

*Dear Jessica,
Happy Reading!
xoo
Tisha Ventu*

Internet Dates From Hell

Trisha Ventker

www.InternetDatesFromHell.com

iUniverse, Inc.
New York Lincoln Shanghai

INTERNET DATES FROM HELL

Copyright © 2006 by Trisha Ventker

All rights reserved. No part of this book may be used or reproduced by any means, graphic, electronic, or mechanical, including photocopying, recording, taping or by any information storage retrieval system without the written permission of the publisher except in the case of brief quotations embodied in critical articles and reviews.

iUniverse books may be ordered through booksellers or by contacting:

iUniverse
2021 Pine Lake Road, Suite 100
Lincoln, NE 68512
www.iuniverse.com
1-800-Authors (1-800-288-4677)

Design and Artwork by Gerald Lee
All illustrations Copyright © 2006 by Gerald Lee

The information, ideas and suggestions in this book are not intended as a substitute for professional medical advice. Before following any suggestions contained in this book, you should first consult your personal physician.

Neither the author nor the publisher shall be liable or responsible for any loss or damage allegedly arising as a consequence of your use or application of any information or suggestions in this book.

The stories that you will read in this book are based on actual encounters that the author has experienced. All specific names, places, and personal information have been changed, and events have been slightly modified for the anonymity and protection of the people involved.

ISBN-13: 978-0-595-39115-8 (pbk)
ISBN-13: 978-0-595-83502-7 (ebk)
ISBN-10: 0-595-39115-X (pbk)
ISBN-10: 0-595-83502-3 (ebk)

Printed in the United States of America

To my husband, Tom, whose constant love and belief in me have made this possible.

Contents

Preface xi

Part I   ***Internet Dates from Hell*** 1

Chapter 1   Talk on the Phone At Least Once Before Meeting .. 3

Chapter 2   Ask for a Recent Photo 7

Chapter 3   Don't Meet Your Date in a Foreign Country. ... 11

Chapter 4   Don't Fall for Someone Just for His Accent. 23

Chapter 5   Don't Waste Too Much Time on the First Phone Call 27

Chapter 6   Always Plan Your First Meeting to Be Forty-five Minutes or Less 31

Chapter 7   If He Still Lives at Home with His Parents, Don't Bother 35

Chapter 8   If You Can't Stand His Voice on the Phone, It Only Gets Worse in Person 41

Chapter 9   Watch Out for Pathological Liars 45

Chapter 10   If Your Date Obsesses over a Body Part, Chances Are He Has a Fetish. 47

Chapter 11   If Your Date Is Flashy or Pretentious, Chances Are He Is Hunting for a Trophy 53

Chapter 12   If Something Smells Fishy, It Usually Is 61

CHAPTER 13	If It Looks Too Good to Be True, It Usually Is . .	65
CHAPTER 14	Be Wary of Someone Too Eager to Travel a Great Distance Right Away	73
CHAPTER 15	Don't Date Someone Who Has Never Been in a Relationship	77
CHAPTER 16	Pay Attention to Red Flags	81
CHAPTER 17	Long Hair Doesn't Always Equal a GAP Model	87
CHAPTER 18	Don't Date Someone Who Lives at Work	93
CHAPTER 19	Don't Date a Biter	99
CHAPTER 20	It's a Small World After All	103

Part II   Hope Prevails *107*

CHAPTER 21	Finally! My Internet Date from Heaven	109

Part III   Posting a Personal Ad *119*

- *Dos and Don'ts* *121*
  - If You Are a Woman Seeking a Man 121
  - If You Are a Man Seeking a Woman 123
- *Helpful Hints* *125*
  - Hobbies and Interests 125
  - Descriptive Words 127

Part IV   Just for Laughs *129*

A Sampling of Responses 131

In Closing 143

Acknowledgments

Michael Gerhardt (Pulitzer Prize nominee author)—for marking up the first pages of this book and providing the necessary guidance and assistance so that I could navigate the difficult world of publishing, and also for being my mentor in this wonderful world of writing.

Becky Moran—for believing in me from the very first time I mentioned this project to you.

John Small (brother and adjunct professor of English literature)—for helping me to appear literate and making me look at the style of my writing in a totally different light.

Roger—for being there for me through all of these crazy dates and still being a wise counsel, best friend, and moral supporter.

Carolyn Sikora—for listening to my endless whining about Internet dating and pointing out what's important in a mate.

Isabella McClancy—for being my ray of sunshine each day at work and for making me feel that I am not as neurotic as I think I am.

Paula Crayon—for always making me laugh out loud and making me be as gutsy as you.

Gerald Lee (artist of the images in the book)—for the amazing talent that you possess and enhancing my book.

Peter Small (brother, aka "Seep")—for keeping an eye on me and protecting me throughout our childhood.

Patrick Ventker (aka Mr. Fantastic)—for always believing and saying exactly how you feel.

Pat and John Small (aka Mom and Dad)—for not freaking out on me after reading this book.

Maxie (my three-pound canine)—for your unconditional love and for keeping my lap warm throughout the endless editing process.

Past Internet Dates—for giving me material and inspiring me to write this book, and for our unforgettable encounters.

Preface

Suppose you are a thirty-year-old single woman living in New York City—the coolest, trendiest city in the world. You would think that this location would offer you the greatest possibilities of meeting the man of your dreams. Well, think again. Even though there are millions of single men living in Manhattan, you really only cross the paths of a few thousand in a lifetime; unless, of course, you change your path and open up endless opportunities. I changed my path, and it truly changed my life.

Take what you want from my story. Whether you are a man or woman, whether you are in a happy relationship or not, whether you simply want a purely entertaining read and have entered the perils of hell in online dating yourself, or whether you are just beginning the journey and need a few tips, my story is a hilarious account of how I became determined to find a mate through Internet dating.

There I was at my parents' house on the eve of my birthday, ready to celebrate. However, unfortunately, I wasn't in the mood. The candle on the Carvel ice cream cake was in the shape of the number thirty, and I was still single. Earlier that day, I partook in a series of self-deprecating comments after getting off the scale for the seventh time. "Why can't I ever get below 158 pounds?" I whined to myself. I wonder what the normal weight is for someone who is 5'10". "I'll never be able to wear those trendy low-rise jeans with this ass!" I mumbled despairingly to myself. Who needs jeans anyway? I can get away with wearing long skirts. Why do most American women, regardless of their shape, rarely feel good about themselves?

My depression was also caused by the fact that I was turning thirty and still had not met a suitable mate. It didn't help matters that I taught kindergarten in a school in the suburbs where all males were either under the age of ten or married custodians. You would think that things might have changed when, only a few months earlier, I had moved to New York City. I thought I would have endless opportunities to date starchy Wall Street suits, hot bohemian artists, Renaissance men, aspiring actors, or Internet start-up moguls. Boy, was I wrong.

Let's step back in time. Let me explain how I ended up in Manhattan. I had grown tired of the endless strip malls and the same old local hangouts on Long Island, where I had spent my entire life. I was ready for the city—the "city that never sleeps." Due to the fact that I still worked on Long Island, I needed to be close to the Long Island Rail Road at Penn Station, so my daily commute wouldn't be horrendous. I called my best friend, Greg, who lived on 34th Street for guidance. Greg told me that it was virtually impossible to find an apartment in the area near Penn Station. Providing I did find one, the rent would be a small fortune. Every weekend, throughout the months of September and October, I scoured apartment buildings on both sides of 34th Street looking for a "For Rent" sign. Not one was in sight. This street separates Chelsea and Hell's Kitchen. *Miracle on 34th Street* was filmed there. Even a model, whose name we'll protect, had her face slashed in front of the Improv in this area, back in the eighties. Although the area was a bit seedy, it was real! For if I were to move to the Big Apple, this area is exactly where I would want to live to get the full experience.

After several weekends of unsuccessful searches, I decided to go visit each apartment building and introduce myself to the doorman. Isn't it always the doormen who know the latest gossip and juice of the building? And another thing—wouldn't the doorman know if there were any vacancies on the horizon? Before I entered, I'd put on my charm, brush my long hair, and refresh my lipstick. I even had my own business card to hand to him before leaving. It's not that teachers normally have business cards; I had actually made them on Broderbund Print Shop for tutoring purposes.

Finally, on the first day of November, when I had nearly given up hope, I received a call from Ralph, the doorman of Greg's building. He told me that an apartment was available on the 16th floor. This happened to be the same floor on which Greg lived. I thanked Ralph repeatedly after he had given me all the important contact information. I wasted no time and called immediately. Before I knew it, Greg and I were neighbors.

A few weeks later, I was a full-fledged resident of Chelsea, New York. I quickly learned that clubs and bars were not the places to meet a quality, marriage-minded man. Of course, living in one of the largest gay communities in the United States didn't help matters either. Nonetheless, I didn't want just *any* man; I wanted an intelligent, educated, thoughtful, self-sufficient, *family-oriented* man between the ages of thirty and forty. People may offer women like me a gratuitous "good-luck girl"; however, luck is not something to rely upon in this situation.

I had never experienced great difficulty in meeting men! "The One," however, simply never materialized. The typical "club type" ranged from twenty-three to thirty years old. Most of these overly confident shortsighted "clubbies" fell short of the mark. One could tell that their intentions were to get their dates comfortably drunk so they could proceed to their apartments for some self-indulgent fun. Many of these men were disappointed when they discovered that women who are determined to find a marriage mate typically drink little or nothing at all. In my experience, determination and alcohol are strange bedfellows, and a strange bedfellow is the last thing a woman like me is looking for.

The gym, like the bar, is not the best place to pursue a mate. To start with, any man who has to check his appearance twice as often as a woman does, begs the question "what the hell is he looking for?" These guys aren't looking for wives! They're already married—to themselves. Another problem with these "gymbos" is that a large percentage of them are not heterosexual. Face it: I didn't have time to convert gay men, nor did I want to! Conversely, the remaining percentage of gymbos seem only to be interested in the feminine loins or rump roasts that these meat markets attract.

Finally, the blind-date scenario. Sometimes setups were simpatico; however, most didn't run smoothly. The chemistry became forced, despite the shared intentions. How many of you have desperately tried to overlook the eighties throwback wearing jogging pants and gold chains, and claiming a "connection" with you, only to wish you were back home with your cat, Erasure CD, and incense? Or have you ever looked for an errant fork to stick in your ear rather than sit for another five minutes laboriously listening to one more sentence about gigabytes and the latest computer geek technology, while your date's unsightly excess hair gel drips onto his lavender polo shirt? I've held out this long; I'm not about to settle now. This is not how I was brought up by my parents.

I was born and raised on Long Island. My father made his living as a bread salesman, each day driving his truck from one food establishment to another selling baked goods to keep a roof over our heads. My mother was an elementary school teacher, much like myself. Graced with three older brothers (if you call that grace), I was the youngest in the family. I had a relatively normal life. I spent my summers at the town pool, when not riding the waves at Jones Beach. Winters were spent making snowmen, when not traveling with my folks to Disney World or the Poconos. Surviving twelve years of private school, I endured the capricious behavior and the overwhelming imposition of self-guilt by the "ladies of the cloth." After high school, I tried nursing school, but hated it. Subsequently, I attended both undergraduate and graduate school in education, earning a bachelor's and a master's degree. If that was not "interesting" enough—for nothing is more boring than learning from teachers who teach teachers how to teach—then the juicy parts of my life occurred much later, especially when I decided to post a personal ad on the Internet. As Dante is warned before he enters the Inferno, "Abandon all hope, ye who enter here!"

PART I
Internet Dates from Hell

1

Talk on the Phone At Least Once Before Meeting

February 1997

I became tired of clubs, bars, setups, and waiting for a "spontaneous meeting," so I began to surf the Web. In the search box, I entered the word "singles," and up came hundreds of singles sites! There were singles sites for lovers of cooking, golf enthusiasts, scuba divers, and ski bums. There were sites for Jewish, Christian, Asian, and Russian singles. Next I tried searching the word "dating." Since I was using AOL, "love@aol" emerged at the top of the list. I clicked on the link and then scrolled through what seemed to be hundreds of ads with photos of both men and women. It looked simple enough, so I posted an ad that day. Since I didn't have a scanner at the time, I didn't include a photo. How bad could this be?

The next day I checked my e-mail, and twelve responses to my profile appeared! All of them looked pretty normal. However, the responses were from men much older than I. My request was for men between the ages of thirty and forty. Of the hits I received, some were from the Midwest, a few from Long Island, and several from New York City, but all were without photos. It now made sense. The sooner I attached a photo, the better the responses would be. From that point onward, not only would I attach photos to my ad, but I would also request photos in return.

Although in my spare time I dabbled in photography, where would I get a recent digital photo of myself? Also, how could I attach the photo to my profile? I had no scanner, nor did I know the procedure. This quandary was soon solved by a visit to my best friend and new neighbor, Greg, whom I've known for the past twenty years. Greg is not only technically proficient in the latest digital photography but is a self-described "Trekkie" as well.

After an hour-long photo shoot in Greg's apartment, he downloaded the best photos—a black-and-white head shot, along with a flattering full-body shot. I was satisfied. The moment I attached photos to my ad, the number of responses increased tenfold. In less than twenty-four hours, I had 144 responses in my mailbox! After reading each and every one of them, I came up with five potentials, two maybes, and 137 deletes.

Of the five potentials, the first was a thirty-year-old architect named Chris who lived in the East Village. Chris's interests included black-and-white photography, golf, cafés, listening to classic rock, and mountain biking. His attached photo was in JPEG format, and he appeared attractive. He had spiky, short blond hair and was standing in front of a famous landmark (the cube on Lafayette Street and St. Mark's Place). Although the sunglasses bothered me, I was intrigued, so I wrote back.

What ensued was an exchange of e-mails lasting a number of days. As a result, Chris expressed an interest in meeting me and suggested a Starbucks located in the East Village. Racked with anticipation, I lay awake the entire night before the meeting. One good thing about that experience was I realized that putting off calling the plasterer was not an option. A once unsightly tiny crack had overtaken my entire ceiling! I realized that I had to tell the newlyweds who lived in the apartment above me that they had better cool it or they would come through my ceiling! Isn't love grand? How in the hell did that ugly little nymph find such a good-looking, polite *acrobat*? Some girls have all the luck.

As I lay awake, my mind wandered. I hope he'll like me and be attracted to me. I hope he won't be put off when he sees that I'm not a size two. What would it be like to marry an architect? Most women engage in imprudent daydreaming; it is a fault none of us can overcome when the possibility of romance is in the air. I was planning our walk-in closets without even meeting him! My mind raced on. I was picking our style of home and community! In my case, imprudence is an understatement!

The next day, fearing tardiness, I barreled down Ninth Avenue to Penn Station an hour before our rendezvous. I was in luck—no sooner did I pass through the turnstile when a C train pulled up to the platform. Reveling in my good luck, I realized that I was heading north when I should have been headed south. I got off at the next stop and proceeded up the stairs to street level, bringing me to the corner of Broadway and 42nd. It seemed like an eternity before the little illuminated man instructed the masses to walk. Did you ever wonder why it isn't an illuminated woman who gives us the "go ahead"? I scuttled down the steps to the southbound E train just in time, and was East Village bound. I got out on 14th Street and briskly walked to my transfer train. As soon as I was comfortably seated, my old nemesis arose again. Damned daydreaming! Now, it was "Josh" if it was a boy and "Karla" if it was a girl! Ironically what brought me out of this next bout of surrealism were advertisements for Internet dating. This particular train car was littered with promos for a matchmaking service only a few blocks east of my destination. After what seemed like eons, I arrived at my stop at Lafayette Street. As I approached street level, I saw the cube (famous landmark), bringing me back to the initial photograph that started this journey. My watch screamed lateness! I briskly arrived at the coffee shop in a fashionably late manner.

As I entered the coffee shop, the aroma of myriad coffee beans filled my nostrils. The sensory overload was rudely overpowered by the loud noise permeating the coffee shop. I couldn't decide what was worse, the sound of the milk steamer or the useless chatter from a table of Goth teens sitting in the back. I chose the milk steamer, as I have been taught to forgive immaturity.

Not knowing Internet dating etiquette, I decided not to sit and wait; I got in line and ordered a cappuccino. As I waited, I turned to face the door. Several men came in, and each time one entered, my heart stopped as I nervously wondered whether each one was Chris. After a few minutes, my cappuccino was ready. Just as I received my change from the cashier, I felt a tap on my shoulder.

"Hey," the person said. The voice was female. I numbly turned around.

"Hi, I am Chris," the woman said. Confused, I replied, "I don't understand. I thought you were a guy!"

"I am not a guy, but if I told you I was a woman, you wouldn't have wanted to meet me."

"Well, you're right. I'm not a lesbian and that's your mistake." I was so pissed that I inadvertently knocked my cappuccino all over the counter, and onto both of our shoes to boot! Realizing my stupidity, I scurried for the door while overhearing Chris yelling, "Don't knock it unless you've tried it!"

To think that I had stayed up late the night before plotting my next course of events and had lost sleep over this date! I felt like a fool. However, when one plays with fire, one gets burned. With Internet dating, the inexperienced cannot only get burned, but also scorched and charred, if not careful.

This concludes our first lesson. Talk to the prospective date on the telephone at least once before going out on a date. If I had done so, I would have detected a subterfuge. I also think I should have asked for a photo taken without sunglasses. People who insist on wearing sunglasses in photos normally are hiding something. When I got home, I wanted to take my ad down and forget the whole damn online dating thing. And get rid of my outdated sunglasses. Yet, as fate would have it, when I opened my inbox, 132 new responses were present! I guess the head shot worked! From this point onward, my technique would be different…

2

Ask for a Recent Photo

March 1997

A month later I adopted a better procedure. Sifting through all the e-mails, I would first read the response and then download the photo. Based on chapter 1's lesson, if a person wore shades in the photo, I would request another photo taken without sunglasses. A day later, I would contact the person by phone if he supplied his phone number. For safety's sake, I would call him from a blocked number. It's a good idea to leave only a few crumbs in the beginning of one's dating trail.

Some have even suggested using *67 to block one's caller ID. In today's world where identity theft is so prevalent, using this method may be advisable.

If the person sounded eccentric or freaky, I would politely excuse myself from any further discussion. If the person was interesting to talk to, I would plan to meet him at a public place such as a diner or coffee shop close to my apartment, so I wouldn't put myself in jeopardy. Being within a three-block radius of your home is a great idea for a first date.

A stage actor named Paul contacted me. He described himself as a six foot one inch thirty-four-year-old living on the Upper West Side. He fit the requirements of my request. As did I, Paul enjoyed travel, biking, and museums. He included two photos of himself. The first photo, a black-and-white head shot, was reminiscent of a young Sylvester Stallone from the early *Rocky* films. This made me a tad apprehensive. I remembered the character as good-looking and dull-witted. The last thing I needed was another good-looking, dim-witted celebrity-like character. What's worse than waking up after five years of marriage to a husband with the intellectual capacity of a twenty-year-old? (Although haven't some of us met some very mature twenty-year-olds?)

The second photo was a group shot consisting of a foursome outside the 19th hole at his country club. Standing third from the left with his arms around golfers' number two and four, he seemed gregarious, athletic, and jovial, which intrigued me. What bothered me was I couldn't discern the year the photograph was taken.

I wrote back to Paul telling him that I liked his profile and thanked him for his photographs (learning from my first mistake, I began to insist on at least two photographs to confirm gender). I also requested his phone number. It didn't take long for him to respond with an e-mail that included not only his cell phone number, but also his home and work numbers. I decided to call him at home in the early evening. After talking on the phone for more than an hour, I found out that the group golf photo was taken a few years back. Although the photo wasn't recent, I went ahead and planned to meet him the next day at a diner across the street from my apartment.

I got there early and took a seat in a booth facing the door so I could see him enter the diner before he would see me. I waited in anticipation for what seemed to be hours, but only five minutes had passed when a huge guy entered the diner, waved at me, and sat down next to me. "Hi, I'm Paul," he said as he picked up the menu. He didn't look anything like his photo. He must have weighed at least 280 pounds, and none of the additional weight was muscle! In the photo he was at least 80 pounds lighter! I didn't want to say anything about his weight, of course, but I had to say something. He also looked at least fifteen years older than in the photos, which perturbed me more! If this is what Internet dating was—deception—I needed to decide whether this was for me.

"Your eyes are even bluer in person," Paul shared. Just when I had generated enough courage to say something, a tired waitress interrupted the moment as she came to our table and said, "What will you have?" I imagined telling the waitress that I wanted the fastest way out of the diner, but instead I ordered a Diet Coke. Paul ordered a cheeseburger deluxe with a side order of onion rings and a chocolate milk shake. I was sure his present weight was a direct result of frequently ordering healthy meals like this! I thought to myself, "Boy, this date will turn out to be over an hour long." Paul didn't even notice that I only ordered a Diet Coke; he was too busy drooling over the food photos on the menu.

I casually remarked, "I didn't recognize you, Paul. Were the photos that you sent me recent?"

Paul immediately responded, "No, they were taken years ago. I look different now because I had to gain a lot of weight for a role I had to play as a Vietnam vet."

"Oh, what was the name of the play?" I inquired. He then told me that he did not remember the play's name. Of course, I knew the whole story was a crock of bull.

I don't believe that I am overly shallow. However, if I'm not attracted to the candidate, we might as well not even meet. I tried to give Paul the benefit of the doubt, asking him about any other roles that warranted a drastic weight increase or decrease to fulfill. To this day I'll never know if he heard my question or not, for no sooner did I ask him than he responded, "Would you reach over and grab that ketchup bottle from the other table? I think ours is empty."

After the date I went home very disappointed and found solace in binging on Ben and Jerry's Chunky Monkey ice cream while opening my e-mail. I counted my responses over the first week. I had received a total of 840 responses and had met two deceitful people—but as I was learning the ways of Internet dating, I realized that there was much more to the equation.

3

Don't Meet Your Date in a Foreign Country

March 1997

A few weeks later, I again perused the subject lines in the sea of e-mails. Here are a few examples: "You Are Hot!," "Nice Knockers," "Hey Babe!," and "Are you a natural blonde?" Just to get a laugh, I opened a few. The rest I deleted right away. I included a sampling of some of the more outrageous responses in Part II (just in case you need a laugh, too).

While scrolling through my e-mail, I discovered one with this subject line: "Englishman in New York." I was compelled to closely examine this response. This respondent claimed to be Simon, although after my first experience with Chris (from chapter 1), I was a little leery regarding "name sincerity." Since the response appeared charming and witty, I responded.

His profile read as follows: "I am a 6'1", thirty-eight-year-old, buff, blond, blue-eyed writer...residing in a quaint cottage in a hamlet within Kent, England." His occupation (although quite obtuse at first glance) was a writer (of what, I still do not know to this day). Although this intrigued me, for I consider myself somewhat well-read and a fair-to-middling writer, I was skeptical because he never mentioned the nature of his writing. Novels? Biographies? Children's books? Self-help books? Comic books?

As a hopeless romantic, I was intrigued by foreign lands and foreign literature. This seemed perfect! However, perfect is a relative term. But I am a sucker for the exotic. Once again, more celestial than earthbound, I neglected to consider the main ingredient—distance! To the Brits, four thousand miles is a "skip over the pond"; however, to us mortal Americans, that is a five- to six-hour plane ride across a turbulent Atlantic Ocean. Not to mention the $2,000 plane fare. Since he gave me a toll-free phone number, I was curious; I decided to call the next morning.

His English accent pulled all the right strings and seduced me. Stating he was only two hours away via the Concorde, he said he would fly in a heartbeat to meet me at JFK. What would I have to lose? We spoke on the phone several times during the next couple of weeks, finalizing the plans for his trip to the United States. I was to meet him at the gate of the flight from Heathrow to JFK. If he was half as attractive as the photo indicated, then this would be a great experience!

I finally discovered the essence of his writing talent during our telephone conversations. He claimed that he wrote political exposés regarding the White House and its internal affairs, as well as other political issues. Wow! A far cry from the comic books I feared he wrote. Although as a child I loved Archie, Veronica, and friends, unfortunately Jughead is the character I most resembled before this debacle ended. I didn't really delve into exactly what he did; I just got caught up in this "James Bond" type and was hooked by talking to him.

When I saw him in the crowd of passengers, he looked exceptional! Staring at his radiant smile, flowers in hand, I nearly fell over someone's carry-on bag. After a polite peck on the cheek, which I felt proved his gentlemanly manner, we collected his bags. I drove him to the Marriott Marquis in Midtown as we exchanged small talk. After introducing him to a few friends, we headed to Central Park for a picnic. Since this was not his first time in the United States, or in Central Park, he knew exactly where to go—Sheep's Meadow. I was impressed! I was so relieved that I had worn my light blue sundress that day, because it was perfect. Although I had an itinerary planned, he took the reins; this too impressed me, for that's exactly what I needed at that time of my life—someone to take control.

By the end of the weekend, his control was dominating. At the airport, Simon bought a first-class round-trip ticket to London for me to use a couple of weeks later. Talk about hook, line, and sinker. I was netted and gaffed before I knew it.

For the next two weeks, I couldn't think of anything but Big Ben, Piccadilly Square, and fish and chips. I even went so far as to listen to old Elton John albums, just to get into the British mind-set. Even the Oxford English Dictionary looked good, for I needed to brush up on my British terminology. Did you know that the English call an eraser a "rubber" and a cigarette a "fag"? I didn't. Nor did I know a bundle of sticks is a "faggot," an apartment a "flat," and a wastepaper basket a "dustbin." Odd!

Minutes before landing, I put on my spectator pumps once again, which matched my stylish sailor dress brilliantly. When I landed at Heathrow, Simon was at the gate, looking exceptional. How he got his teeth so white, I'll never know. We loaded my luggage into the car and spent the remainder of the day in London. We even stopped to "take" high tea with scones and fresh cream. At that point I felt strangely like a Charlotte Brontë character, except that I had everything I wanted.

But nothing could have prepared me for what came next. After a wonderful day we went back to his so-called "cottage," which was actually an English Tudor mansion! I was so jet lagged that I went to sleep in one of his many bedrooms, which was actually an apartment containing a dressing room, a parlor, a lavatory, and a view of the veranda. I was thankful that he truly was the gentleman he portrayed.

The next day we enjoyed muesli and cream and took a ride to Canterbury, where we experienced the beauty of the cathedral where Chaucer's pilgrims journeyed, the burial site of Saint Thomas à Becket (the blissful martyr), poet's corner, and a plethora of enchanting country roads and village shops. Before we knew it, even Simon admitted we were lost and I believed him. You might think this was the oldest trick in the book, like an American high school boy running out of gas to cop a feel or, as the British put it, steal a peck. Nevertheless, we were indeed lost! As we veered down one country road after another at a very comfortable speed of forty miles per hour, I never felt apprehensive or worried, because both Simon and the Jaguar were handling the situation brilliantly. The bucolic scenery was breathtaking.

Finally, after forty-five minutes of enjoying the views, Simon recognized more of a road than the dirt paths we had been traveling on. As if Chaucer himself were personally guiding us, we found ourselves at the outskirts of London, at the threshold of The Tabard in Southwark. For some reason this ancient public house intimidated me. Simon's explanation clarified why. I was where the pilgrims originally departed from in Chaucer's great story. Amazed, I marveled at the excellent quality of the building's restoration. I couldn't wait to get inside, where I was transported back in time. It was no longer the twentieth century. Although the people were dressed in twentieth-century garb, eating and drinking in front of me, the surroundings took me closer to the fourteenth century. At the waitress's insistence, we ordered bangers and mash and, for dessert, a slice of pork pie. Even though the English are known for bland food, I truly enjoyed these dishes. It may have been the company, the surroundings, or both, but I have never looked at sausage and potatoes the same since. After great post-meal revelry (guitars and English country folk ballads), we booked the last two rooms that The Tabard had available.

After the customary English farewell, we thanked the host and headed north to York to meet Simon's dad. At this point, Simon alerted me that the drive was about three and a half hours from Southwark to York, but he assured me that it would be worth it.

As our drive commenced, Simon was right to ask whether I had slept well. I felt extreme fatigue without any reason. In the midst of one of his sentences, I think I fell asleep. Blame it on jet lag, the lush countryside, the antiquity of Southwark, or a combination of the three. I could've sworn he told me his father had left his mum for his kindergarten teacher. My slumber must've been only minutes long, because when I awoke he was still talking, not even realizing I had dozed off. The topic was still his family, so the jury was still out on whether he had said that or I had imagined it.

Simon was right; it was three and a half hours to York. After approximately three hours, he told me it wouldn't be much longer. We turned onto yet another country road, and he told me to look for an imposing eight-foot stone wall with a wooden shingle reading Kensington Manor. Finding it, he turned left through an enormous arched wrought-iron gate, which seemed to be hundreds of years old. The scroll on the shingle was calligraphic. It too was not of this century, or even of the last two. Even the wood itself seemed to have endured at least two hundred years of English rain and snow. As we drove between two gargantuan hedgerows, which seemed to run for miles, Simon's jack-o'-lantern grin frightened me. Talk about a Brontë novel, this was far more ominous than anything Jane and Catherine, put together, had ever experienced. As the hedges disappeared, the house was remotely visible at the end of two rows of about a hundred yards of enormous Norway maples. I hesitantly looked to the right at Simon, hoping the grin was more Cheshire-cat at this point. I was relieved. His face was as normal as I knew it in the brief time we had spent together. I decided it was a good time to refresh my lipstick. Circling the enormous fountain and listening to the crush of

English limestone under the Jag's tires, my apprehension faded, and exhilaration returned.

Staring at the enormity of the edifice, I didn't realize that Simon had opened my door. How in the hell did he turn off the ignition, exit his side, circle the car, and open my door that quickly? Needless to say, there was something wrong here.

Before I knew it, two servants materialized on the top steps outside the front entrance, beckoning the two of us forward. A third mysteriously appeared from behind the car with our luggage, asking Simon, "Did ya *have* a lark, Mr. Simon?"

"Most definitely, Albert. Please show Ms. Patricia to the vestibule; thank you," Simon said.

As if in a dream, I was whisked up the stairs with Simon nowhere in sight. When I asked where Simon was, Albert grinned at the other two elderly servants, and they returned stoic glances. Once inside, I truly realized the garish wealth of this family. Adorning the vestibule wall were life-sized portraits of the Kensington men dating back hundreds of years. Oddly, each face was relatively similar: their apparent evolution was more static than any other family I have ever seen. As I ambled through the vestibule, awestruck, I approached Simon's portrait. It was Simon as I saw him in the present day, not advanced in age like the others. When I turned to ask Albert about the odd nature of the portrait, I found myself virtually alone at the end of the vestibule.

Controlling my inordinate fear, I reexamined the portraits and concluded the following: these men looked eerily similar. Even the tuft of hair on the bridge of the nose was perfect in each of the likenesses. However, the most disturbing factor was the sardonic smile each possessed; it was too much like Simon's smile once he saw the Kensington Manor shingle. No sooner had I pondered this thought than a voice interrupted my concentration. It was the voice of Simon, Sr.

"Welcome to Kensington Manor, Ms. Patricia. May I be of assistance?" I realized immediately who it was. With the exception of the gray hair, he was a mirror image of Simon.

"It is a pleasure to meet you, Mr. Kensington," I responded.

"Lord Kensington, if you please," he politely demanded.

"In that case," I replied, "just call me Trish." He frowned. He looked down at the Italian marble floor and muttered something indecipherable. At that point his wife emerged, or, if you will, stumbled through the doorway.

"So I hear you're from the States," Dame Kensington mumbled. It was apparent that she had had way too much to drink by two o'clock in the afternoon.

"I'll leave you two birds to chirp," Mr. Kensington reluctantly retorted. As he walked away shaking his head and nervously spinning his pinky ring on his left hand, I still wondered where Simon was.

Dame Kensington added, "Do you know Sandra Bullock, dear? I just loved her in *The Net*. How about Sharon Stone? Wasn't she divine in *Basic Instinct*?"

Before I could answer her slurred questions, Simon finally appeared, dressed like his father. What is it with these guys with their smoking jackets and ascots in the middle of the day, and their nervous fidgeting with the pinky rings on their left hands? Before I could answer Mrs. Kensington, Simon grabbed my arm and rushed me through the double doors, leaving her asking more American movie star questions.

"I am sorry you had to see that, Trish, but there are better things ahead," Simon insisted as he escorted me down a hallway lined with stone statues of mankind's greatest philosophers from Socrates to Descartes. Before I knew it, we were in a hall obviously used for dining. Although the table was at least twenty feet long with as many chairs, there were only four place settings apparent at the far end of the table. When I asked Simon if his father and mother would be joining us, he despondently replied, "My father will eat, but his wife will only drink."

As the three butlers pulled our chairs, Mrs. Kensington who had followed us demurely down the hall, asked me whether I wanted gin or vodka in my martini. When I told her I seldom drink, she shriveled her mouth and said jokingly, "Right. That leaves more for me." I could see Simon was obviously embarrassed, so I felt the necessity to compliment him on his jacket. Before I could speak, Mr. Kensington entered the room, followed by two cooks and two waiters. The first cook had an enormous silver-covered platter; the second cook had a tremendous tureen with a ladle attached to its side. The waiters carried champagne and wine. Dinner consisted of a roast with rosemary potatoes and carrots. The soup was a light broth, and it all tasted otherworldly.

During the entire time, Dame Kensington got sauced on the gin martinis that she incessantly drank as she rambled on about American cinema and the superior films we Yanks produce. Sensing further embarrassment, Simon interjected that I happened to be a kindergarten teacher and loved my work. I noticed Mr. Kensington's face drop as his wife blurted forward, "Isn't that a gas? So was I when I met Mr. Kensington. What a lark! Simon, Jr., happened to be my star pupil. Although Simon was brilliant, Simon's father insisted I enhance his giftedness." For the next hour, no one spoke except Mrs. Kensington about her failed attempts at elementary education for the children of York. It seems that once she met and married Mr. Kensington, the community abandoned their respect for her.

When he wasn't staring a hole into his roast, Mr. Kensington was staring a hole into me. He was making me very uneasy. Thank God he didn't try to repeat history with me!

Just when my trepidation reached its peak, a clock rang twelve bells. Almost robotically, everyone seemed to move on cue toward his or her respective bed chambers, as did I. I felt hypnotized as if a force much greater than nature was in control. Simon automatically retreated, barely saying good night. After one of the best sleeps I have ever had in my life (or as a rock in the Hudson, as we Yanks would say), I awoke to a very changed Simon and family. Mr. Kensington, Mrs. Kensington, and Simon were all casually dressed at the dining table, which starkly clashed with the way they appeared the night before. After a typical, curt English breakfast we were on the road again, yet this time with less conversation and more driving.

After about ten minutes I broke the silence with the same question he asked me after The Tabard, "Did you sleep well last night?" He responded with an abrupt no and with nothing more. During the drive, I made up my mind. Forget the looks. Forget the intelligence. Forget the wealth. This family had serious issues. All of a sudden we were pulling through the gates of a much different estate. The wooden cattle guards and swinging gates made me feel much more at home. Hopefully the people here would be as different as the surroundings. This time there were no hedgerows, Norway maples, and no crushed limestone, but just a gently winding dirt road, which comfortably led to a modest farmhouse. Within seconds, a kindhearted-looking woman of about seventy opened the door. Even from the distance of approximately one-hundred feet, I sensed compassion. Her blue apron with three little ducks stitched to the pocket convinced me of a sense of sincerity that was lacking in the last home. For a second I thought I was in Ashroken, Long Island, not in Leeds, England. When she waved to us with both arms above her head, I truly felt at home. It almost reminded me of my nana, and the way she used to greet my brothers and me. This time, Simon didn't open the door for me. He walked somberly, head down, to his "mum," almost pretending that I didn't exist. Although they embraced, it wasn't warm and close. They patted each other on the back respectfully as if they were old war buddies who hadn't seen each other in twenty-five years. I found it disturbing, but far less so than the scenario that I couldn't wait to escape just an hour ago.

At that moment a second woman appeared, a little larger than the first, with a similar apron; hers was red with a hunting scene of a fox being chased by dogs stitched on the pocket. Ironically they both looked alike. I don't know why I fixated on their aprons, but anything was better than those horrific portraits and statues in the Kensington estate. Both women looked exceptionally healthy. As it turned out, they were sisters who found solace in each other's company twenty years after failed marriages. Joan, Simon's mum, and June, her sister, each had one son. June's son, Nigel, had served as the British consul to the United Nations. He now owns a rather lucrative sheep farm in Devon. At this point Simon realized I was still in the car and scurried to introduce me to his mother and his aunt. As soon as I entered the house, June invited me to sit at the kitchen table. The sisters were making pies and stew on a tremendous six-top wood burning stove. I have never seen anything like it in my life. The smell of the wood burning was incredible; no Christmas yuletide or campfire came close to the comfort this cooking fire provided. Joan joined us quickly, apologizing for taking so much time.

"No matter how many times Simon visits me, he always forgets flowers. He's up on the hillock picking some wild ones for me and his aunt," Joan expressed. June snickered as she stirred the stew pot, warning Joan to check on the pies. Once Joan opened the oven doors, the aroma sent me reeling.

"Cherry and apple," Joan said smiling. "Happen to like cherry, dear?"

"Sure, cherry is my favorite and apple a close second," I replied.

June said, "She'd fit in here like a hand in glove, wouldn't she Joan?"

"She's always welcome to visit us." Joan responded.

Joan finally dropped the bomb. "I take it you just came from Kensington Manor?" Joan asked with a face as serious as the estate itself.

June followed, "What did you think?"

"I really haven't had much time to think about it. However, I feel much more comfortable here," I cautiously responded. After a quick glance at each other, the ladies roared laughing, and I fittingly joined them.

Joan reminded me, "We don't let just anyone sit at our kitchen table."

They laughed in unison even harder. Before they could stop, Simon entered the door with two bouquets of flowers. Like a ten-year-old, he offered his aunt and his mother the bouquets. I wondered why he didn't bring me any, and as if by magic, his mother questioned him on the same subject. His response was as cold and calculated as I could have imagined. "I picked the hill dry, Mum, and there's not a pansy left." I thought, "Now if I only could get rid of him and coerce one of these fine Englishwomen to drive me to Heathrow, I could save this vacation." No dice! As fate would have it, neither of the women drove.

During small talk over stew and cherry pie, Simon floored me as he jokingly referred to me as his "potential future wife." I almost choked on the piecrust! His mum laughed and replied, "How daft. Have you neglected to tell her all those crazy monster stories of yours, Simon?" Simon brushed it off and laughed uncontrollably. That made me curious. What monster stories was she talking about? Should I be concerned? When I questioned the ladies and Simon about these monster stories, they changed the topic as fast as an English rain.

Bidding them farewell, I promised them if I was ever in Leeds again, I would pay them a visit. I had a wonderful time, and I thanked them sincerely. Simon did also; however, this time he had no hug, no pat, but just a handshake for both mother and aunt. This regression of sorts perturbed me.

As we backed the car into a U-turn, I glanced to see both women once again waving with both arms overhead, while Simon stoically concentrated on the drive home. I asked him, "What monster stories are they referring to?"

After a few moments of contemplation he just replied, "It is too risky for me to get into. The fact that I even took the chance to come to the United States to see you was like suicide."

"I think I have the right to know," I responded. "After all, you referred to me as your future wife."

After a pause he divulged his secret. "Look, dear, there's a price on my head."

"What in the hell are you talking about?" I demanded.

He proceeded to tell me that he had lived in Los Angeles for a few years, and he had been married to an American girl. He said he had gotten into some things and the U.S. government had pursued him. "What things?" I insisted. More silence. Then he continued to share. They had put him into an American jail for a few months. I asked him what kind of stuff he was into. He told me that he was educating the people on covert government operations in Washington, D.C. "Like what?" I asked. It only took one question and Simon spoke for the next two hours. He spewed the following craziness to me:

1. Washington, D.C., is led by an evil social order, established several hundred years ago, whose insignia can be found on any U.S. currency. This group holds most of the power and influence not only in our government, but also in other governments all over the world.

2. Our current president is the Antichrist and his wife is a full-fledged witch.

3. The New World Order directly correlates to World Government Fronts. They have training centers for a global army of psycho-social agents, which are groups that house the masterminds of global transformation strategies.

4. The obelisk (Washington monument) is demonic and was made to be a phallic symbol, sarcastically symbolic of the male-dominated society in which we live. The entire layout of Washington, D.C., is serpentine, representing the earliest known earthly vision of the devil.

I was stunned. I didn't know whether to laugh or ask more questions. Because I am a very curious person, I decided to ask more, and he obliged.

5. The microchip is the beginning of the end. In the book of Revelations, it states that the end of the world will come when the government forces the people of the world to implant a chip into their skin so that every person's move can be watched. He referred to it as the "Big Brother chip." This is the way for them to track our lives, including our identities, our bank accounts, our experiences, our plans, our dreams—everything.

"What does this all mean?" I asked.

He replied, "Your government is a representation of the devil! This society is a direct link to the ancient Wiccas, Babels, and Tummuz, which spans thousands of years."

"How come I've never heard of this?" I asked.

Simon responded, "Most people don't know that in 1776, a man named Adam Weishaupt founded the Luciferic order, which was created as a special order meaning 'ones with light,' signifying its members had been initiated into the secret teachings of Lucifer, the supposed 'light bearer.'" I was both intrigued and afraid. I asked Simon to tell me more. He went on to say that there were conspiracies all over America. He added that the New Mexican government is hiding seven strands of aliens in the desert.

"How do you know?" I inquired. He told me that he has videotapes to prove that aliens exist. He mentioned Amazons, Green Men, and aliens like E.T., among others.

There I was in England, 4,000 miles away from home sweet home, listening to all of this freaky stuff. I didn't know what to do. I had planned to be in England four more days. How would I get out of this one? What do most people do when they need help to get themselves out of a mess? Yes, they call their mother. That night I called my mom when Simon was asleep, and I told her to call back first thing in the morning to say that I needed to return to the States immediately due to a sick aunt. "I told you so!" my mom replied. "They're all nuts on the Internet. Should I call the police?" I told my mom I would be OK and would take necessary precautions. First thing in the morning, I'd get my ass out.

I couldn't sleep that night for obvious reasons. As a periodic insomniac, my remedy has always been reading. Silently I made my way downstairs and stumbled upon Simon's library, which was filled with many marble notebooks. Each notebook was labeled with a different conspiracy in handwritten thick black marker: "Armageddon," "The JFK Conspiracy," "The Beginnings of Witchcraft," and "Top Secret: Aliens and the Government." Not only my spine, but also my spirit became chilled. At first I thought the chill was due to England's damp, cold evenings. However, I quickly realized that meteorology had nothing to do with it. The nature of these innocent-looking schoolgirl notebooks was anything but innocent or elementary. I hastily made my way back up the stairs, double-locking the door as I had promised my mom.

The next morning my mom called as requested. Simon answered the call but only spoke with her briefly before handing me the phone. I exclaimed with an "oh my goodness" and "will she be all right?" several times. After concluding my phone call, I told Simon that I had to get the earliest flight home that day, due to my aunt's illness.

I managed to board the 4:01 PM out of Heathrow for a change fee and ticket price difference. None of that mattered, though. While driving to the airport, Simon insisted that I marry him, move to the United Kingdom, and stay with him until the end of the world. It was at that very moment I knew that this book was eminently necessary. Neither Poe nor Hawthorne could write a story like this. Ironically, to add even further drama, at that moment the radio announced that the Comet Hale-Bopp had been in the sky the previous night and that the Heaven's Gate cult had committed suicide in their Nikes and purple shrouds in California. Another chill ran up my spine.

I prayed that I would get to the airport in one piece. When I was on the plane, I ordered a shot of sambuca (even though I rarely drink) and tried to forget my nightmare.

How could a fairy tale turn into a gothic nightmare? As I sat there and stared at the seat in front of me, it all came to me. Evil can compete with evil. Goodness doesn't compete with evil; it prevents it. Evil is hereditary. I wondered what I could have done differently to avoid this situation. I realized I didn't ask Simon, early on, exactly what he did professionally, and if I had delved more deeply, I would have found that he really didn't work, but was financially supported by his father. His writing was just an eccentric outreach to protect his old-world order from being threatened by the new. Once again, I should have been more of an investigator. I also didn't ask many questions up front about Simon's beliefs, spiritual ideas, and significant events in his recent past. I was too caught up with the romantic fantasy to be concerned with the facts. I've always been known to take chances. My philosophy is that if you don't take chances, you don't live life to the fullest. Conversely, if you have the misfortune to encounter the wrong person, you subject yourself to real danger.

Thankfully, I arrived safely at JFK and had to endure a half-hour lecture from my mom about the losers found on Internet dating Web sites. Simon called me a few times after my adventure in England. He wanted to know if I had decided to take him up on his offer and move to Kent. I told him that I was happy to live in the United States, and he admonished me that I would go down with the rest of the "bloody Americans" and hung up.

4

Don't Fall for Someone Just for His Accent

February 1998

You would have thought I would have learned my lesson after the England escapade with Simon the previous year; however, another appealing man wrote to me, but this time the locality was Perth, Australia. It's funny, for I always had an affinity for the Australian accent. After a number of e-mail exchanges, I offered David my cell phone number, since I wasn't about to call Australia. Immediately David struck me as funny, witty, and persistent, from our initial telephone conversation. During about three weeks of conversing, I posed very detailed questions about his life in Perth. I even took notes and would occasionally revert to them with additional questions. His Aussie accent sounded like Mel Gibson's. All I could see (in my narrow-minded, smitten way) was David driving an olive green outback-type jeep, navigating through the tall grasses of the Australian bush country. Exactly what he was pursuing didn't matter, although I hoped it wasn't some defenseless koala that had strayed from its litter. In the long run, it would have been better if he had pursued a koala, compared to what he ended up pursuing.

Included in my ad were my favorite things (koalas, spicy tuna rolls, sunflowers, a fresh box of crayons, log cabins, and beach sunsets). In response to the ad, he hastened to include that his favorites were somewhat similar to mine. He too liked koalas and beach sunsets, since Perth is surrounded by water. However, spicy tuna rolls and crayons elicited question marks. It was only later that I regretfully had the opportunity to qualify my penchants.

Trying desperately to impress me (and he damn near did impress me), David proceeded to mail a box to me at the address I gave him. Feeling wary about divulging my home address after my experience in Kent, I gave him my brother Peter's address instead. A few days later, Peter called me to inform me that David had sent me a package via first class mail. I asked Peter to open the box. Since he didn't know what the box contained, he sounded rather tentative. In fact, he gave me hell for arranging that a package be sent to his address. Being used to digesting tablespoons of hell, I swallowed this one because my brother was right that I should have forewarned him. Regardless of his cynicism, I convinced him to open the package. As he proceeded to cut through the packing tape, he shouted, "You're crazy. What if there is a bomb or some other device in here?" A few minutes later he told me that David had sent me a stuffed koala bear, a can of tuna fish, a box of jumbo crayons, a tiny Lincoln log cabin (which he carefully glued together for shipping purposes), sunflower seeds, and a postcard of a typical Australian sunset. I thought this was so sweet. Later that day, I picked up the items at Peter's house. At the bottom of the box, I found a heartfelt letter and photos of David's children and home. I actually had no idea that he had children, since he had never mentioned them before.

After much contemplation I decided that didn't matter, and I would not prejudge a man because he had children. I also decided that I wouldn't let miles, differences of race, religion, or nationality stand in the way of meeting my soul mate. Shortly thereafter, I called him to thank him for the package, and at that moment, he asked me how daring I was. You should never ask me that, because I take on most challenges. He asked if I would be up for traveling if he sent me a first-class ticket from New York City to Perth, Australia. I told him the England story and explained to him that I would never again go to anyone's home. He then offered me an alternative plan, suggesting we both fly to a halfway point—Hawaii, for example. I told him I would arrange for accommodations in separate hotels, so if things didn't work the way I planned, I would have a safe haven to which I could retreat. I thought this was a reasonable plan. He stipulated that if I didn't like him, then I could be on my merry way and have a free flight to Oahu. I replied, "It's a deal!"

Because it was winter break, school was out. Flying to Los Angeles, and then catching a connecting flight to Oahu, all the while enjoying first class, I came to the sudden realization that this could be fun. No sooner did I allow myself latitude and premature levity than that old bugaboo of mine raised its ugly head again; it was that sense of dread and trepidation! Although the fine meals served on the flight distracted me, I wasn't going to allow my vision to be clouded.

Overhearing a snobby couple bickering behind me, I pretended to peruse the menu. Dressed from head to toe in ill-fitting Gucci garb, these two cartoon characters were more entertaining than the inane film shown on the flight. I don't know what was worse—her peach lipstick or his spray-on tan? I am sure that she was with him for nothing more than the size of his wallet. But then again, in today's world, it's possible she was the one with the money. I finally engulfed myself in some Céline Dion music available on one of the airline channels and reread the safety card from the seatback pocket (where else would you put that air mask that drops down, other than on your face?). At times like these, my mind wanders into its own Aussie territory. After the announcement to push up the tray tables, I quickly brushed my hair and checked myself in my small pocket mirror. What if he is not attracted to me? What if he likes his women thin? The old self-deprecating thoughts quickly reemerged. We finally landed, and as I exited the airplane, I quickly scanned the crowd for my Aussieman.

The music stopped, the crowd parted, and there he was, with a bush hat and all. Just kidding. I saw him approach me, and I noticed that he looked at least fifteen years older than his photo. Like Paul (the mistake in chapter 2), David had tried to pull a fast one by sending me an earlier photo of himself. However, this time I wasn't safely across the street from my apartment building. Although he was attractive, I neither heard bells and whistles nor did I see fireworks. But maybe that was a good sign, based on my past experiences.

It also appeared that he wasn't too enthralled with me. I didn't see his eyes light up once he saw me. Perhaps I too looked older than my photo or he didn't realize until he saw me in person that I was a few pounds overweight. But he was pleasant nonetheless. Separately we both had arranged our lodging. The hotels were conveniently located across the street from the airport.

Over the next two days we engaged in several platonic activities such as sightseeing, ocean swimming, and a day trip to Kauai. After swimming, I wondered if he was put off by the sight of my body in a bathing suit. Although he was pleasant and extremely cordial, we both knew the error of our ways. Without saying it, his nonverbal expressions exuded his error. His eyes were aloof, his voice was monotone, and the incessant tapping of his fingernails at the restaurant table communicated a clear disinterest in me. I too began noticing single men my age everywhere I went, and I half-wished I was talking to them instead of David. Although I increasingly felt I was with a brother rather than a potential mate, I became quite comfortable with David.

After revisiting his original intentions in Internet dating, I discovered why his first and second wives had divorced him. Ironically, it was due to chronic infidelity stemming from his Internet encounters. Talk about clouded vision. After more than a half an hour of David's lurid tales of sexual fiasco, I noticed a slight tear developing in the corner of his right eye, as the traditional Hawaiian sun shower emerged. I then truly realized that the Internet dating world was an extremely sharp two-edged sword; David cut himself free from two marriages and three children, yet he also continued to cut short any chance of future happiness. As far as I was concerned, the only knife I was interested in was a single-edged knife (a machete, maybe?) that could cut me a path the hell out of there!

David finally showed his maturity when he shook my hand the way men ordinarily do, and apologized to me, yet another innocent victim. Both the revelation of his infidelity and the heartfelt apology cleared the path I needed. Boy was I glad there was no initial spark. We mutually agreed there was not a match there, and we both went our separate ways to enjoy the remainder of our vacations independently.

During the flight home, I began to question why I kept doing the same thing over and over again. Why do I have a love of adventure and a need for excitement? What makes a man from another country or state any more interesting that the ones who live close by? Why do I risk my health or safety in embarking on these encounters when deep down inside I have doubts? One word comes to mind: hope.

5

Don't Waste Too Much Time on the First Phone Call

October 1998

After an eight-month hiatus from Internet dating, I decided to repost my profile and give it another go. Saul, an American Jewish cosmetic surgeon wrote me a lovely letter accompanied by what appeared to be a recent photograph. I say recent because you can never be too sure (right?). He was attractive and bright-eyed, so I felt compelled to give him my phone number. By the time I returned home from work, Saul had called twice. No sooner had I changed into my jeans and T-shirt, than the phone rang. It was Saul. Instinctively, I looked at my kitchen clock, then my answering machine, then back to my kitchen clock, all the while talking to Saul and walking from room to room. He had called three times within the last hour! The first call came forty-eight minutes earlier, the second, only eighteen minutes ago. This unnerved me. I received three phone calls in one hour. Like in the cartoons, I felt a tiny little poke in my lower neck (remember that little red devil with trident in hand, perched on one shoulder, and the angel with the harp on the other?). Well, the poke I felt was not from an angel's harp!

I could have easily jumped to conclusions, like I have recently trained myself to do, and categorized Saul as nothing more than a desperate nutcase responding to a photo of me. Magically I heard the angel's harp all of a sudden in my left ear. So I chose to give him the benefit of the doubt. After all, he was a surgeon. Maybe he was between surgeries or patient rounds and he stole an hour to reach me. That's normal, right?

The conversation began in the sweetest of ways. "I hope I am not disturbing you. This is Saul, you remember, right?" How could I not remember, when he had left two messages thirty minutes apart, and no one else had called me that day, which was a dry day for me.

"Sure, Saul. How are you? I got your messages, and I was just thinking about you."

"Really, that's reassuring."

Reassuring? I had found a cosmetic surgeon with self-image issues? If so, we had that in common. Maybe he had just chosen the wrong words.

After an hour and ten minutes of verbal volleyball, I gathered the following information about Saul. He was a forty-one-year-old cosmetic surgeon, educated at NYU, and had recently completed his fellowship at NYU Medical Center. His favorite things were playing and watching hockey, attending the opera, wine collecting, and playing tennis. He resided in Greenpoint, Brooklyn, and was unmarried but had hopes of marriage in the future.

The phone call flowed so well, I was eager to meet him. I painted this mental picture of him as we spoke. I pictured him somewhere between Ben Affleck and Harrison Ford, with an air of professionalism apparent.

We planned to meet a few days later outside a café in the West Village, for Sunday brunch. Since our conversation had gone so well (and was inordinately lengthy), I agreed to a meal date as our first meeting. As I approached West Tenth Street and Greenwich, I asked the cab driver to drop me off a block or so before the café. I needed at least a block's walk to gather my thoughts. Also, during that short stroll, I might catch a glimpse of him from a comfortable distance. As fate would have it, that is exactly what happened! He was exiting his brand-new BMW right outside the bistro! I stopped dead in my tracks. So abruptly, that the woman behind me pushing her child in an open stroller smacked into my Achilles tendons. While we exchanged polite apologies, I somehow lost sight of him. Obviously, he had gone in. With less than half a block to go, the little pitchfork poked me in the neck again. What was wrong with what I just saw? What was it about his physical characteristics that shook me? Was it his legs? Was it his torso? Was it his head? I just couldn't put my finger on it, but I decided it had something to do with his head.

Instead of proceeding directly to the restaurant, I crossed the street and found myself in front of the Traveler's building. I pretended to hail a cab. As cabs came and went, I tried desperately to see through the 8×12 window sashes to confirm my doubts about Saul's head. Once again, fate was on my side (if only that damn devil would stop poking me in the neck and the angel would start strumming a tune). Saul took the first table just to the right of the entrance, street-side. As he feverishly paged through the wine list, it appeared as if he were wearing a toupee. From my vantage, it looked more like a piece of romaine lettuce than a bad rug. Oh no, I did it again! What the hell—what are a few follicles between friends?

My hand was still in the air, and a cab pulled up. The cabbie yelled, "Where to, Miss?" I almost broke out laughing. The cabbie had the worst wig I had ever seen. I had to put my hand on my mouth to stop my hysterical laughter. I mustered enough composure to respond, "I changed my mind. I think I'll walk." At that point, the cabbie yelled, "What is it? My aftershave ain't cuttin' it fer ya?" If only he knew.

As I approached the restaurant, Saul recognized me, waved through the window, and pointed to my seat. I did everything I could not to stare at his head, although I knew I would have to make eye contact sooner or later.

In a polite, gentlemanly manner, Saul bolted upright and pulled out my chair before the waiter could do it. He said I was right on time. He added that I was even prettier in person. He took the liberty of ordering two glasses of Santa Margarita Pinot Grigio. Remembering his love of wine, I didn't argue. Up to this point, I had carefully avoided looking at his head. I realized there was quite a draft and I couldn't determine its origin. It certainly wasn't coming from the doorway because this month of October was unusually warm. I looked around and noticed an enormous oscillating fan above our table. Saul seemed pleasant, but still his hair looked funky and I wasn't sure what it was.

I ordered eggs Benedict, and Saul ordered bagels with lox. When our dishes arrived, he looked as if he was sweating from nerves. I told him not to be nervous, and he told me that he had an anxiety disorder and felt nervous in new situations. At that moment I looked down at my eggs Benedict and saw that it was covered with black pepper. I even blurted out, "I didn't put any pepper on the eggs. What the hell is this?" I then looked up, and he excused himself, saying he had to go to the men's room. As he nervously stood, I could see his hair flaking off into my eggs Benedict! His so-called hair was actually spray paint! I thought those infomercials in the early hours were a hoax! I never thought in a million years that people actually used those products! I honestly could not eat my brunch after seeing his sweaty fake hair flake onto my eggs. What a waste!

He must have had a little can of touch-up spray-on hair because when he returned from the restroom his head looked back together (whatever that might be). I played with my eggs while he was gone so at least it looked like I had eaten some. I felt really sorry for Saul. He was a nice and accomplished guy, but this "wig in a can" was a real turnoff. I just wanted to go home. I offered to pay, but he wouldn't allow it. I thanked him and hailed a cab home. He wrote me a few more times and I just kept answering that I was busy. I hope he reads this someday and decides to shave his head instead of wearing that awful spray! Anything is better than that aerosol nonsense.

If I spent less time daydreaming about possibilities during our first phone conversation and more time studying his recent photograph, I would have determined a touch-up job had been done. Altering photos with a computer is a ploy in Internet dating deception.

6

Always Plan Your First Meeting to Be Forty-five Minutes or Less

December 1998

Less than two months later, another physician responded to my profile. This was Angelo, a five foot eleven inch behavioral psychiatrist who resided in the East Village. He sent a photo. The photo was far more definitive than any I had received to that point. By "definitive" I mean that it was clear, like an old Polaroid, except the date and time appeared in the bottom right-hand corner. Although the image portrayed him as balding, he didn't attempt to hide it in any way—no spray-on hair. Learning from my mistake of looking but not seeing the image in the photograph, I studied this one carefully. With time and date as a great help, I stopped wondering when the picture was taken and focused on the particulars.

Unlike the others, which were obviously taken twenty or thirty feet away from the subject, this was a close-up, taken from eight or, at most, ten feet away. Seated on a group of rocks, Angelo was waving to the camera. He was flanked by enormous oak tree trunks (definitely a rural area). I thought he looked rather cute in his denim jacket and black boots. However upon closer analysis, I noticed in the bottom left-hand corner of the photograph what appeared to be the curve of a motorcycle's rear fender, red light, and New York license plate. Was he into motorcycles? Nonetheless, he looked in good physical condition despite his hair loss, and his smile was inviting. I thought that there was something different about the watch on his left hand. With my knowledge of computer photo imaging (thanks to my friend Greg, whom I mentioned in the preface), I zoomed in to Angelo's left arm, but it still appeared unclear. If only I knew then what I know now regarding computer imaging.

After responding with a detailed profile, I sensed sincerity on his part and therefore concluded that we had a lot in common, so I took his number and gave him a call. We had a great phone conversation, in which we discussed his love of opera, ballroom dancing, travel, scuba, and exotic cuisine. He also talked about the yearly renaissance fairs in which he actively participated. "Hmmm," I thought, "he's an intellectual and an M.D., and a lover of the arts and medicine. Adding to my intrigue, he mentioned that he treats his women well (although I didn't know if I liked the plural form "women"). He stated that he loved to pamper his lady. It sounded too good to be true. I asked him how he pampered his lady, and he responded that he liked to give massages, brush her hair, do her housework, etc. This time, Old Man Reason was knocking on the doors of my perception. Knocking may be an understatement; he was downright banging this time. If only I had invited him in.

We planned to meet at the famous Russian Tea Room in Midtown Manhattan. Although I thought I would be the early one, he arrived first. When I asked him how long he had been waiting, he demurely responded, "Twenty minutes, not long at all, my queen." I didn't know which was more bizarre—the way he responded or the way he was dressed. Covered in leather from head to toe, he painted more a picture of a motorcycle club member than a behavioral psychiatrist. Jacket, pants, boots, and even a leather shirt was a bit over the top! I wondered whether his socks were made of leather, too, and where was that silly Village People hat that would complete this look? I didn't need to look for the Harley; I knew it was outside somewhere. Or was it?

It didn't take long for me to confirm that Angelo was indeed an M.D. because I was a nurse before becoming a teacher and I knew medical terminology. We discussed psychiatry and different medications for disorders. We compared notes regarding great sites for wreck and reef diving. We even discussed the best places for Turkish cuisine. He also confided in me concerning his previous girlfriend, who had a borderline personality disorder. After a while, I decided to ask him why he was dressed in full leather garb. He responded, "I'm going to a ball."

"Don't you need to wear a tuxedo to a ball?" I asked.

"No, I am going to a 'black and blue ball' downtown later."

I asked him what a black and blue ball was. He told me that it was a fetish party for people who liked to be told what to do. I asked him where in my profile it remotely indicated that I might be interested in that sort of activity. His response was that since I was a teacher he thought that I would be great at disciplining him! Hence, the leather wardrobe! I then proceeded to ask him what motivated him to be subservient or dominated by the objects of his affection. I discovered, during over an hour of painstaking digging, that his mother was overly domineering. Consequently, in his frantic search for a match, he only looked for women in authority, be it anyone from kindergarten teachers to CEOs of major corporations.

His good old mom was anything but a woman of real authority; her idea of discipline was sensory deprivation. For something as menial as breaking a glass or tracking dirt into the house, Angelo and his sister were locked in a dark closet for minutes on end. For something more heinous, like failing an arithmetic exam or wetting the bed, the tub water would be drawn with exceedingly hot water and the children would be forced to sit in it for inordinate amounts of time. God forbid they broke her cardinal rule, which was talking back to any adult or challenging an adult's authority in any way. Angelo's mother would march them down to the basement where two three-foot speakers and a lone chair sat. Once seated, operas from Verdi and assorted other famous conductors were played at unhealthy levels of volume. This could go on for hours, depending on good old mom's demeanor. To this day, I think about Angelo and the extremely appropriate occupation he has chosen, and I hope that by helping others, he may find a way to help himself. It was at this point that he decided to don a pair of sunglasses, which solved the mystery concerning what I thought was a watch on his left wrist. The letters "S.M.S.O.A." were clearly visible on the stainless steel bracelet on his left wrist. What made matters worse was that beneath the bracelet the same letters were tattooed across the inside of his wrist. He noticed me staring at both bracelet and tattoo, and offered the meaning of the acronym. He explained that the letters stand for the Sadomasochist Society of America.

After all of that, it is hard to believe that he asked me if I would like to accompany him to the S&M party that night. I never even addressed his question nor offered an answer. I politely excused myself to the ladies' room to plan an escape. No sooner was I in one of the stalls than I instinctively looked at the ladies' room window, which was too small for me to escape through. The most mature and humane thing to do was to be honest and tell him that he had made an error. I was not masochistic, sadistic, or any other "-istic" he was looking for. Much to my surprise, after all this delaying, when I returned to the table, Angelo had vanished!

I received a strange voice mail that went as follows: "Hi, Trisha. Sorry I had to run, but if you change your mind and would like to have your house cleaned, give me a call."

Although for a second I actually thought my house certainly needed a good cleaning, my common sense quickly resurfaced. I decided to do it myself, thank you very much.

Here is a suggestion: Tell your Internet date that the first encounter can only be forty-five minutes long, due to a previous appointment that you had forgotten. It could be a handy way to escape this type of date from hell. On the other hand, if the date goes positively, this will entice the person to call for another date at another time in the near future where more time can be spent.

I had met a few people in between the dates up to this point who were either not what they portrayed themselves to be or not interesting enough to read and write about. The whole process was just fascinating. Each and every person opens up a new world to explore. Dating a myriad of men is like a smorgasbord. It was extremely entertaining, and it made for a much more interesting life than a grade school teacher would normally be exposed to. When would this searching end? Would I ever find contentment with a "normal man?" Since I had encountered a majority of unique individuals, would I be bored with a "regular guy?" I was always drawn to exotic men, either exotic-looking or from another culture. Although I have dated American men, it is the exotic men who intrigue me. When I am out with a man from another country, I feel like I am away in that country. In my teaching career I have three months of vacation every summer, and I have used this opportunity to travel extensively around the globe. I have more passport stamps than a seasoned diplomat. There is nothing I enjoy more than seeing the world. I am simply seeking an intelligent man with whom I can travel, learn from, be inspired by, and inspire. Why is it so difficult?

7

If He Still Lives at Home with His Parents, Don't Bother

January 1999

As I mentioned before, deception comes in many shapes and sizes. It's important to note at this junction that a person may not be purposefully deceptive if he is indeed deluded by grandeur. Obviously, each person has a different sense of the reality that surrounds him or her. Homes (like shapes and sizes) can be viewed differently by different people.

Todd's e-mail seemed humble. Although he mentioned that he worked at a local power plant as a "troubleshooter," his schedule was flexible. As a thirty-five-year-old, he claimed to own *two* homes, rent an apartment, enjoy hunting and fishing in the Poconos, and restore old Broncos from the eighties. He also noted that he found me very attractive and thought I resembled a young Catherine Deneuve. Periodically I would get compared to Stevie Nicks from Fleetwood Mac or the French actress Emanuelle Beart. Both, I took as a compliment.

At first blush, Todd seemed as rugged and outdoorsy as any of the previous candidates. Deception, however, loomed largely, later on in our brief relationship. Todd looked very attractive in the photo he attached to the e-mail. He looked like a darker version of the Marlboro man, without the mustache.

The first phone call went well. Because of the first, we spoke a few times the next day. The only thing that bothered me throughout the duration of these four phone calls was his insistence on talking about his mother. I don't know why it bothered me, but it did. In my home we were brought up to respect our mother. Very infrequently, if at all, have I ever heard one of my brothers speak badly about our mother. As a matter of fact, when the matriarchal topic arises in conversation, my brothers are quite positive with their assessment about our mother. So why would this bother me? I finally decided to meet Todd at the Tick Tock Diner on 34th that I used to frequent (by the way, it makes the best Greek salads).

After two dates, I was mildly intrigued. The third date, however, did not go as well. We found ourselves en route to Home Depot. As an avid apartment dweller for the past ten years, I rarely found myself at home centers. My shopping haunts were more on the department store level, so this kind of store, too, was new to me. Before I knew it, we were in the window dressing section, in an aisle full of vertical, Venetian, and even beautiful mahogany wooden blinds. Instead of consulting me on fabric or color or window treatments in general, Todd excused himself politely and phoned his mother. Although he was a good eight to ten feet away from me, I could hear every word he spoke. Occasionally, he glanced in my direction to see if I was listening. During those instances I pretended to fidget with the bolts of vertical blind fabric. His words included, "But, Ma, the dimensions of a window is height and width. Just measure the width of the sill and the length of one of the sides of the window. Come on, it's not that difficult. Call me back!" "Isn't that nice," I thought. "His mother is helping him redecorate his apartment." I wished we were all that lucky. He returned somewhat red-faced, apologizing politely. I said nothing. We exchanged smiles and browsed through the variety of blinds available. Less than five minutes later, his cell phone rang again. "Ma, again, just measure the width and the length! It doesn't have to be perfect, just give me a rough idea of the opening."

He looked over at me with head tilted to one side and smiled wryly. Ironically, an announcement over the PA system reported that a little lost boy had been found and was eagerly awaiting his mother at the courtesy desk. I couldn't help but make the association regarding Todd. Nevertheless, I mentally plodded onward, trying to stay positive.

A week after the "Home Depot incident," I found myself in a late-eighties semi-restored Bronco on the way to the Poconos. Todd alerted me that he had a lunch planned at his country home. He talked so much about this home that he led me to believe this was a quaint, warm, vacation getaway. Just then his mother called for the third time, and we hadn't gone ten miles. "Yes, Mother, no need to remind me who owns the home. I know you and Dad purchased the home before I was born. You don't have to remind me."

Todd admitted at that point that he didn't own the home; it was his parents'. Alright, a little white lie wasn't going to interfere with this date. However, with a hundred miles to go, I estimated that his mother would call at least six more times. She actually called seven!

We finally pulled into a small rural town, one and half hours from New York City. What bothered me was the rusted sign attached to an even more rusted pole adjacent to the dirt road where we turned left. What confused me even more were the twenty or more rusted mailboxes under the Etonia town limits sign. As we pulled up the driveway of the development, I saw structures behind a group of trees. It looked as though someone was shooting a movie there.

I asked Todd, "Is there a documentary being filmed here?"

He responded, "What do you mean?"

"What's with all the trailers?"

"Those aren't trailers. Those are country homes."

For the next ten minutes I observed the most bizarre campground I have ever witnessed—not that I am a great camper or anything. These were not quaint homes! They were trailers, damn it! No matter how hard some of the families tried to decorate the outside of these "homes," the decorations still appeared contrived to me. My jaw ached. I must have had my mouth agape for ten minutes. When I finally mustered enough nerve to look at Todd, he was red-faced and appeared irked. His silence was deafening. At that moment, I felt that the appropriate thing to do was to apologize for my astonishment. No sooner could I mouth the words, then I was completely overwhelmed by not one, not two, but six enormous plastic pink flamingoes posed to drink from some nonexistent oasis in front of a metallic-type home. These trailers looked more like spaceships than did the rectangular-type box homes that we had passed over a quarter of a mile before. My consternation increased dramatically from this point onward. What would be beyond these otherworldly looking homes?

After what seemed like forever, we finally approached Todd's "vacation home." There were no flamingoes here, but just used car parts strewn everywhere, including tires painted white, with enormous weeds growing out of the middle.

Wildlife seemed to be hopping from one truck part to the next, and I hoped it was only squirrels. My jaw began to ache in conjunction with the migraine I was developing. As if in a dream, Todd appeared at the front door of the trailer. I didn't even recall him turning the engine off, leaving the vehicle, and walking the fifty or so feet through the waist-high grass (damn daydreaming again!). The grass looked as though it hadn't been cut since the previous fall. When I saw him gesticulating to me to get out of the car and come into the house, I wanted to run (in the opposite direction). God knows what was in that thing! All I could imagine was a variety of fishing rods and reels, hunting equipment, old newspapers, dirty dishes, and a television that dated back to the fifties. What I encountered next was far worse (if you can believe it).

Dodging at least a dozen of what appeared to be Sunday newspapers (yellowed from the sun and elements) and two extremely large transmission yokes, I finally made it to the front door. Todd was busy straightening up as I walked into the kitchen. I was right! There were dirty dishes, old newspapers, and open tackle boxes, and shotgun shells graced the kitchen table. As if things weren't bad enough, then I noticed, above the sink, a cat's hatch built into the kitchen window. In the corner of the kitchen were two litter boxes filled beyond comprehension. The stench was overwhelming to the point that I quietly gagged. It was incomprehensible why Todd didn't go right to the litter boxes first, rather than removing the empty beer bottles on what appeared to be an old lineman's spool. Doing the best I could to not look at the litter box, I proceeded down the hallway and found a trailer full of mango and avocado-colored leather furniture (definitely sixties), stuffed animals (and I don't mean teddy bears), and that fifties television *avec rabbit ears*. I went to inquire about the squirrel and raccoon on smaller spool end tables, but Todd was nowhere to be found. It was at that moment I saw on the wall a certificate of completion from the Jarrett Taxidermy School of Greater New York. Great, another Norman Bates, right out of the movie *Psycho*.

"Trish, I'll be out in a minute. I am having trouble finding the plunger. If these toilets aren't flushed at least once a week up here in the winter, the line freezes." That was it. I was having trouble breathing, my throat began to close, and hives appeared all over my hands and arms. I had forgotten to remember in all of the confusion that I am highly allergic to cats. I decided to make a dash for the door. To hell with Norman's plunger and his psycho madness! I was out of there! I made it in seconds to the car, despite the auto parts obstacle course. I was proud of my speed and agility.

I realized my anger and disappointment could not win, for my allergies had beaten them to it. Todd must have heard the door slam, because he was behind me yelling,

"What's the matter?"

"Antihistamine," I replied, "I need an antihistamine immediately!"

"You mean aspirin," he responded.

"No, I need an antihistamine." Just then I realized that I keep a variety of remedies for headaches and such in a small vial in my purse.

"Your face looks really swollen. Should we go to a hospital?" Todd inquired.

"No, this antihistamine is time-released and will kick in soon. I'd prefer that we head back to the city."

The hour and a half drive to the George Washington Bridge was in utter silence. Blame it on his embarrassment or on a combination of my anger and my allergies, but neither of us talked. Just as we approached the tollbooth, the silence was broken by yet another phone call from his mother. My mind was made up. I fixated on the long line of cars in the cash lanes as we breezed through the easy-pass lane. In fifteen minutes I would be home.

We crossed the bridge and headed onto the Henry Hudson. The fast journey home came to an abrupt end as the Parkway was completely traffic laden. It was then that Todd began his string of apologies. It was comforting to know that he had some modicum of conscience. He told me that his involvement with Internet dating was his mother's plan, and he had never intended to engage in it. He said that since his father died, he had been extremely shy around females. Since he was an only child and his mother was husbandless, she was reluctant to let him go. When I asked him when his father passed, he astounded me with the answer: "when I was sixteen years old."

He proceeded to tell me that for the last nineteen years he had lived in the basement of his mother's home. He worked as a computer tech, specializing in troubleshooting for the power plant. Since his mother feared lifelong loneliness, she agreed to help him find a marriage partner quickly, so they could all be one happy family. Apparently her dream was to have Todd and his family live in the upstairs of the home, while she took the basement apartment. It struck me then that that was why she was so involved in the redecoration of the basement.

Although sorrow was my first emotion for him, and for his mother too, common sense was in the forefront of my thinking. Before we knew it, we were in front of my apartment building. I prayed that he wouldn't ask me for another date. My prayers were answered. He apologized one more time, and mentioned that if I was ever in the Poconos, I should look him up. His strange laugh made me feel uneasy because I wasn't sure if it was sarcastic or sincere. At least I was home, I was safe, and I could breathe again!

8

If You Can't Stand His Voice on the Phone, It Only Gets Worse in Person

April 1999

Obviously the experience in chapter 4 with David from Australia wasn't enough. I needed another dance with accents. Subsequent to my experience with Todd, I removed my profile for a few months. Time off from these experiences was what the doctor ordered. That year's spring was cold and rainy, which allowed me the opportunity to catch up on my reading and educational research. I couldn't remember the last time I curled up with a good novel, or laughed at some educational reformer's diatribe regarding the preschooler's academic disposition. There were two inches of accumulated dust on my portable rowing machine. So after a couple of months of exercising (I lost ten pounds) and literary pursuit, I felt mentally and physically strong enough to reenter the restricted waters of singles bars and clubs. After two weeks of that nonsense, my fingers again found their way back to the world of the Internet.

There were a couple of definite no's, including one in which a woman requested that I write to her incarcerated brother as a pen pal. Then a neurosurgeon from India who was currently residing in an affluent town in Connecticut answered my ad. He stated that he was 6', thirty-three years old, and the head neurosurgeon of a prestigious university hospital in the metropolitan area. Although Rishy stated he was thirty-three, his photograph indicated a much older man. I chose to overlook the possible age factor, due to his deep sense of spirituality with the written word. I really liked the fact that Rishy responded in conjunction with my interests.

When we finally spoke on the phone, his thick foreign accent made me think of my friend Akbar, the manager of a local Indian cuisine restaurant from which I frequently order takeout. The accent was so familiar that I almost interrupted Rishy with, "Light on the curry, please." Although I was not overwhelmed by his accent at first, it became quickly clear to me that telephone small talk can be totally different from prolonged face-to-face conversations. I thought I could overlook the unpleasant voice, so I decided to give it a go.

To no one's surprise, Rishy appeared in front of my apartment in a brand new Mercedes SL and, wouldn't you know it, it was my favorite color, black on black (although I've been told that black is not a color, but the absence of all color). Wearing a leisure suit with a polo shirt (as if the leisure suit wasn't bad enough), I realized that this man was old enough to be my father. The only thing missing was my father's Old Spice aftershave with the little sailboat on the bottle, although I wished he had some cologne on because he smelled like mothballs. He asked me where I'd like to go.

I responded, "To Akbar's, of course."

He responded, "Is it Indian? It doesn't have to be, you know."

"I love their Indian food, plus Akbar is a friend of mine." I replied.

No sooner did we sit at an available table, then Akbar greeted us and asked if there was anything he could get us from the bar while we waited for our waiter. Without warning, Rishy ordered for the two of us, never asking me what I wanted. Realizing that many foreign men were like this (especially older ones like Rishy), I accepted his traditional gesture. By the time Akbar returned with our drinks, Rishy had told me that he recognized something in Akbar's intonation.

"I am willing to wager he is from New Delhi."

"Why do you say that?" I inquired.

"His inflection is of New Delhi."

Serving us our drinks, Akbar asked Rishy if he was from northern or southern New Delhi. When Rishy responded northern, Akbar promptly sat down at our table. He snapped his fingers twice and our waiter appeared at our table. Akbar ordered the same drink as we were drinking and went as far as ordering our meals. I quietly acquiesced. I thought to myself, "The drink is one thing, but the entrée also?" Well, Akbar knew me, so I wasn't apprehensive.

The men downed their drinks in some odd measure of bravado; I was neither impressed nor interested in it. They then promptly ordered more drinks, both by snapping their fingers. Until that point I hadn't touched mine, so I thought it might be due time that I did. I raised the glass to my lips, smelling it before I tasted it. It was the most awful stench from a liquid I have ever experienced, save the time I inadvertently mistook my uncle's glass of scotch for an orange soda. Taking the slightest of sips, I immediately put my glass down, because this was the most potent drink I had ever tasted. All the while the men talked in their native language, which seemed to thicken with every sentence they spoke. By the meal's end, Rishy was so drunk that his speech was incomprehensible. Between the accent and idiomatic traditional expressions, which he now was insistent upon using, I was befuddled. When I interjected at times for clarification purposes, he became angry. I pleaded with him, "No offense, but I have no idea what you are saying." At this time Rishy became irate. The last thing I remember before leaving the restaurant was Akbar calming Rishy down by imploring him loudly to lower his voice. After walking several blocks and passing some belligerent homeless drunk, I decided to choose safety and hailed a taxi (if you can believe there is refuge in a New York City cab). I told the driver, who was coincidentally also of Indian descent, to take me to 34th Street and 9th.

He said, "You are on the 34th Street and 7th Avenue."

"I know, I'm just not in the mood for dealing with anymore drunks tonight. Maybe you can answer a few questions for me if you don't mind."

He quickly replied, "Certainly, Miss," so I asked him:

"Are you from New Delhi, and if so, from which part, north or south?"

"The south, of course. I drive a cab," He responded.

He proceeded to tell me that those from the north are traditionally affluent. He said he was glad to be from the south, where equality between the sexes reigned. If it wasn't for the poverty level, southern New Delhi would be a beautiful place to live. He finished by saying that in a little over a year he would have enough money so that his family could move to New York. Although he had an accent, not once did I have trouble understanding this man. He spoke the proper English to which I had grown accustomed. After paying him, we said our goodbyes and my spirit was lifted. Little did I think that a southern New Delhi cabbie would raise my spiritual awareness more than Rishy originally intended to. In the elevator of my apartment building, I realized this was the most intelligent conversation I had had in some time. If only Rishy had been half as eloquent as my cabbie friend, then who knows how different that date would have been. It's funny to think of the nerve of that neurosurgeon!

9

Watch Out for Pathological Liars

May 1999

Thirty-year-old Rob contacted me next. He mentioned in his e-mail that he was a Hawaiian-born investment banker. Although his piercing black eyes were quite attractive, there was something deep in those eyes that bothered me. It wasn't until the conversation on the phone that I realized what it was. It began as small talk and chitchat until the topic of birth arose. When he asked me where I was born, I told him in Mineola, New York. He responded with a cute, "If there is a Mini-ola, is there a Maxi-ola?" When it was my turn to question his location of birth, I realized what was in those eyes. As I previously mentioned, deceit can come in any form or fashion. This time it was in his answer. His answer was, "I was born on the island of Kona." I responded, "I beg your pardon—the *island* of Kona?" "Yes," he answered curtly. It was at this point that I either told him of my recent trip to Hawaii or was about to tell him. No matter which, Rob quickly changed the subject. He wanted to meet me next Thursday evening, since Friday he had to attend a banking conference at the Jacob Javits Center. He suggested that we meet for coffee at a local coffeehouse close to my apartment.

No sooner were we served then I realized his attractiveness superseded his photograph. If nothing else, he was a fine piece of eye candy. Even the way he dressed was impeccable. His designer shirt brilliantly matched his pants and leather loafers. He must have been an athlete because of his muscular physique. I couldn't help but daydream.

Sometimes when something bothers me, I have little control over how it manifests itself. Since this was one of those times, I point-blank asked the question again.

"Where did you say you were born?"

"The island of Kona. I thought we discussed this over the phone."

I inappropriately laughed, to which he reacted: "What's so funny?"

"I'll beg your pardon again, Rob, but I've been to Hawaii several times. Kona is a city on the island of Hawaii."

At that point, Rob's sharp eyes grew dull. He said he had a confession to make. He looked embarrassed. He confessed that he was actually Filipino. Before he could say anything else, I asked him if there were any more confessions. He said, "As a matter of fact, there are. I am not an investment banker; I am a teller-in-training. I am taking a couple of undergrad finance courses at NYU. They happen to be both on Friday nights." He looked at my face for my response and I gave it to him, more in words than in countenance. I said to him, "I don't like to be fibbed to, lied to, or betrayed in any way. It is late. I must be going, good night."

Although I myself never played much baseball, my two older brothers sacrificed a set of knees each to that sport. The principle they always talked about was three strikes and you're out. I knew there were more strikes in Rob's repertoire, but I wasn't going to give him more than three.

10

If Your Date Obsesses over a Body Part, Chances Are He Has a Fetish

June 1999

After the last incident I decided to take another hiatus from Internet dating. For what amounted to only three and a half weeks, my respite was well deserved. As any elementary school teacher knows, the last month of the school year can drag on unmercifully. Between final assessments (academic and deportment) and every imaginable fund-raiser and year-end party with my colleagues, the last three weeks can feel like months. What seems to compound matters most is the heat. Long Island summers come fast and furious, once the calendar reads June. Those cool, wet May afternoons quickly acquiesce to unbearable humid June mornings where kids seem to melt as fast as jumbo crayons errantly left on a windowsill.

Nothing is more satisfying than handing the final report card to the last kindergartener and subsequently watching her hand the report card to her all-embracing, patient mother. Marked by the little departure tears from most of my students (unlike the separation-anxiety tears for their parents that they displayed in the beginning of the year), June 25 is a noteworthy day for all elementary school teachers. It is on that day that we, like the kids, have mixed emotions. Part of us craves the idea of a ten-week summer vacation, but the other part spells "emptiness," as we pack the last box of chalk away in our closets. The last thing I needed were mixed emotions regarding my social life, too.

Normally the drive to Manhattan from the middle of Long Island during off-peak hours takes approximately sixty minutes, but before I knew it, I was in the elevator to my apartment. How did that happen? I have heard drunks talk about automatic pilot, and I've also read about road hypnosis while driving, but this was something entirely different. My mixed emotions practically erased the entire drive home. Maybe this phenomenon prompted me to revisit my old habit of Internet dating. Let's face it: watching those young mothers near or about my age jubilantly jumping in the schoolyard alongside their children threw my maternal instincts into an emotional tailspin. The older I was getting, the more intense this feeling was growing. I really felt it was time that I had a little jumping bean of my own.

Like the phantom ride home, I soon mysteriously found myself fingering the computer keyboard, activating my personal ad once again. Within thirty minutes, Francisco, a self-proclaimed Mexican-bred classical pianist answered my ad. Phew! That was fast! I think that was the quickest reply I'd ever received after posting an ad. Maybe I was being overly dramatic, since it had been over four weeks since my profile had last been viewable. Before long I found myself responding. My normal practice is to not give my phone number, but to receive the man's phone number and call him. No sooner did he give me his number, than I phoned him. I learned quickly that not only had he recently recorded his own CD of original music, but he was also working on a second CD of legendary standard tunes. His voice complemented the photo that was attached to his e-mail. But, as most Internet daters know, photographs can be deceiving.

With a soft-spoken, sexy Hispanic accent, he asked if I was available that same evening, since he lived in the same neighborhood, he could be over shortly to meet me. I told him that even though I wasn't busy, it had been my last day of school and I needed to decompress; a container of Ben and Jerry's Chunky Monkey, or possibly Cookies and Cream, some cool jazz, and the latest tabloid would do the trick. I told him that perhaps we could meet up the next night. We agreed to meet for a light bite and early show at a jazz club in Tribeca.

Fashionably late is not the order of business in a jazz club, especially for the early show. He had said 9:00 PM, and it was precisely 8:50 PM when I walked through the doorway. Thank God that I didn't wear heels because these clubs could be so dark that I could foresee falling down the first flight from the street and never being noticed. Little did I know that the sandals I wore would save me some serious time.

Rather than join the huddling mass at the bar for their last drink before the show began, I decided to take a table close to the stage, but not too close for comfort. I can count on two hands the number of jazz clubs I've visited. I was concerned that he wouldn't find me, but that concern vanished when I saw him talking on stage to the bass player as he tuned his final string. Within seconds, he eyed my table. Within a nanosecond, he was seated next to me.

"I had another table in mind, but this is just as good," he initially offered.

"We can move," I suggested, "I'm not married to this spot."

"No, no, this is actually better. We have a better view of the piano player," he said in an unmistakably articulate accent.

He looked much more attractive than the photograph attached to his e-mail. I couldn't determine the color of his eyes, but they appeared, in the darkness of the club, to be as dark as his hair. His clothes, too, were black: a black open-necked shirt, black jeans, and a black sport coat. I'd like to be able to say that he also wore black shoes, but I thought it would be inappropriate to stare at his shoes. Even if I had, I probably couldn't determine it, because of the lack of light. This didn't stop Francisco, though, because before a note was played on stage, he was trying to note my feet (staring no less!).

"Did you drop something on the floor?" I asked.

"Excuse me, what did you say?" he exhorted.

I repeated, "Did you drop something? You seem to be preoccupied with the floor."

"Oh no," he laughed, "although it's a bit dark, I was admiring your feet."

"My feet or my shoes?" I urged.

"Your feet," he quickly offered.

Like most women, I'm sensitive about various parts of my body. However, I can't ever remember my feet embarrassing me. "Feet don't fail me now," I laughed to myself. I pursued this issue without haste.

"Do you have a foot fetish?" I innocently blurted.

"As a matter of fact, I do," he smiled. At that moment I was positive he was joking. I started to laugh out loud.

"What are you laughing at?" Francisco inquired.

"I thought you were pulling my leg—no pun intended!"

"No, I actually have a thing for feet," Francisco retorted.

Great, he was another eccentric.

At that point I nervously laughed out loud again because I realized I hadn't had a pedicure in over a month.

"What's so funny now?" he demanded.

When I told him of my nail neglect, he challenged, "Every foot is different. Some look great with pedicures, some look great without."

"What do you mean?' I said.

"Here, I'll show you."

In one hand he held the table's candle, and in the other hand he held a digital camera and scrolled through dozens of photos of women's feet, which he claimed to have taken that day alone!! You might have heard of "saved by the bell." I was saved by a set—an extraordinarily long set of instrumental jazz music that fascinated "Francisco the Foot Man." Before the set was over, I politely excused myself to go the ladies' room, which is apparently taboo, yet Francisco's fixation on the piano player was undisturbed by my leaving. Before I knew it, my open-toed shoes and I were at the Duane Street platform, eagerly waiting for the train to arrive. Once aboard the train I found myself curiously staring at women's feet. What is it with these fetishes? While concentrating on feet, I realized that I actually found most women's feet quite disturbing to look at. With a size ten shoe and flat feet to boot, I never had the problem most women suffer from, which is insisting upon squashing their feet into shoes way too small in a vain effort to prove that their feet are actually smaller than they appear. Let's face it, there's not much you can do with a size ten. I would rather be comfortable than vain in that department. I choose other areas in which to be self-conscious.

Feeling a well-deserved sense of emotional soundness, I climbed the subway stairs to 34th Street. For the first time in a long time, I felt rather good about myself. If I remember correctly, Francisco did say he admired my feet and was not repulsed by them, didn't he? Therefore, I thought at that point that I'd take his bizarre compliment positively. Don't we all enjoy a compliment once in a while, even if it is backhanded (there's no such word as back-footed, is there?)?

Once again, like in a dream, I appeared in my building's vestibule. It was like that the whole week. Fragments of time seemed to escape me while I safely persevered.

"You look a tad frazzled, Trish," my good-natured doorman, Ralph, said.

"No, just a little spacey the last few days," I replied.

As I said this, I thought I saw Ralph's face twitch as if he suffered some strange pang of discomfort or even downright pain. "Are you all right, Ralph?" I inquired.

"Oh, I guess, it's obvious."

"What is?" I urged.

"Oh, these damn new shoes my wife insisted I wear are killing my feet."

At that moment I broke into uncontrollable laughter.

"I guess you don't like them either, do you?"

I never answered him. I walked to the elevator with my arm above my head waving back to him, giggling like a child. I honestly could not have another conversation about feet that night, for all the shoes in Imelda Marcos's closet. I apologized the next day for my rude departure, and even went as far as explaining myself to good old Ralph, and I called in an appointment to Natalie's Nail Salon for both a manicure and especially a *pedicure* as well.

11

If Your Date Is Flashy or Pretentious, Chances Are He Is Hunting for a Trophy

September–December 1999

Every September, school starts and teachers must leave the summer behind. It normally takes both student and teacher a good three weeks to settle in. With no indication of autumn in sight (because Long Island is notorious for Indian summers, sometimes lasting until the beginning of November), I found myself, for the first time in many years, not only comfortable with my new class and my old principal, but also with my even older single status.

Although the days were getting shorter, it was warmer than most Septembers had been in recent memory. Unfortunately my apartment building super jumped the gun. He ordered his staff to turn off the building's air-conditioning and begin the heating season by the first of October. Here it was Saturday, October 9, eighty-three degrees with the sun blazing, and I was stuck on the sixteenth floor of an apartment building with no air-conditioning. Worse yet, my apartment was on the 34th Street side, directly facing the noonday sun. My Saturday cleaning chores had to wait until the evening. In the elevator I had a very unique thought: rather than another senseless movie or even more senseless shopping spree, I decided to take a cab to the New York Public Library. My brother John had always recommended classic American and British novels for me to read. I haven't had the heart to tell him I don't have time for long boring novels and I am at least a half-generation younger than he. Another thing is that he teaches college literature and I teach kindergarten. His reading is much different from mine. However, ironically I couldn't sleep the night before because of the heat. At 2 AM I found myself sitting in front of the television watching the late, late movie, *Breakfast at Tiffany's*. This was an early sixties film based on Truman Capote's novel of the same name, which John suggested I read. He thought the character Holly Golightly would amuse me because of her penchant for the finer things in life. After enjoying the film tremendously and understanding why John connected me and Holly, I headed toward the New York Public Library to read the book. It has often been rumored that the New York Public Library has one of the best air-conditioning systems of any public building in New York. Even if I couldn't finish it in one sitting as he claimed I would, I could borrow the book and finish it at my leisure. I really loved the story, and if the book were half as good as the film, I would call John and tell him so.

In fact, I didn't finish the book, and I used my library card for only the third time in two and a half years of living in the city. Walking down Fifth Avenue with a library book under my arm made me feel like I was back in high school. This elevated feeling made me giddy. It was truly an innocent experience, because I realized at that point I had forsaken one of the great arts, namely literature, for the others. As an avid photographer, theatre lover, and art museum patron, I realized what was missing in my artistic life. Classic literature, one of the oldest art forms, is an ingredient not to be omitted from the recipe of one's artistic life. I couldn't wait to get home and sit in front of that old box fan and try to finish *Breakfast at Tiffany's*. As I opened the door to my small apartment, which was more of a convection oven since the temperature was still eighty-six degrees at 5:05 PM, I noticed my answering machine blinking. I wondered if that was Marc returning the call that I had left for him earlier this morning.

Marc responded with a photograph depicting a well-built, dark-skinned, dark-haired diamond dealer from Westchester County. His bio revealed an Italian-Israeli heritage with a flair for the exotic. Upon closer inspection of the photograph, I noticed he was wearing neither an ordinary suit nor ordinary shoes. It appeared as if he had four rings, two on each hand, and none of which were in the wedding category. What confused me was the sparkle emanating from one of his ears. What sized diamond earring would make that glare in the photograph? But there was more to look at in the photograph. As much as I like a well-paved driveway that accommodates a foreign car, this appeared to be over the top. His brand-new S-class Mercedes was sitting on a quarry-tiled circular driveway in front of two Doric columns straddling a marble staircase. To top it all off, everything looked immaculate.

I discovered that Marc was an avid New York Yankees fan. It could be coincidence or the power of suggestion regarding his appearance, but I thought that he was a dead-ringer for Yankees shortstop Derek Jeter! He was drop-dead gorgeous! He probably dates model-types, I said to myself. For a few minutes I felt the insecurities creep in. Marc displayed a great sense of humor over the phone. The conversation flowed and was quite enjoyable, so we planned to meet the next night.

He insisted on picking me up in front of my apartment. Going against my better judgment, I agreed. I guess it was that magnificent car or that suit that persuaded me, but nevertheless, I'm sorry I did. He seemed a bit pretentious at first, when he pulled up in his Mercedes, blaring disco music and wearing color-coordinated shades. He was overdressed, to say the least. His behavior was also more pretentious than it needed to be. I hadn't gotten out of the building before Madeline, a big-chested model-type tart, who lived in 12A, was leaning over the passenger's side admiring the upholstery. I stood there bewildered. I felt invisible. Although I had recently lost ten pounds, I was feeling self-conscious. The only thing I could see was that diamond earring and those pearly white teeth smiling at Madeline, as if he had certainly been down that road before. After what felt like an hour, but was only a couple of minutes, I ventured forth.

"Good evening, Madeline, nice sweatshirt. Were you running?"

"Only errands, Trish. Does he belong to you?" she demanded.

"Belongs is a strong word, Madeline."

"Well, ciao for now. Have fun. Bye, Marc." Madeline said.

Hmm, it only took her a couple of minutes to get his name. I wondered what more she got. I realized I should have met him at the restaurant.

"You two acquainted?" Marc asked.

"Like oil and water," I retorted.

Marc laughed—or shall I say snickered? This behavior unnerved me. He didn't know me well enough (or her for that matter) to find this amusing.

"You're beautiful," Marc said.

"Thank you," I responded.

"Nice to meet you, Trisha," Marc added.

He had all the earmarks of a player: well seasoned, well dressed, and quick moving. I decided to divert his attention from good ole Madeline and compliment him on his car and attire. Puffing up more like a blowfish than a peacock, he displayed an ego the size of his bank account. I thought he would ramble on endlessly with self-adulation as the core but he surprised me. For the entire ride to Celeste's in Little Italy, he wanted to talk only about me, my family, and my aspirations. I guess first impressions aren't always correct.

Believe it or not that was one of the best evenings I had had in recent memory. Celeste's isn't one of those typical Italian restaurants where you're seated at white tablecloth glass-topped tables with gratuitous fake flowers in a cheesy plastic vase. Celeste's is renowned for its Italian home style atmosphere, which includes a nightly party. For those unfamiliar with Italian home style, there is no menu and no individual seating. Patrons sit at long wooden tables on wooden benches next to strangers. Everyone eats what is prepared that evening, which is posted on a chalkboard outside on the sidewalk. The walls are bedecked with photographs of everyone from Charlie Chaplin to Robert De Niro, past and present patrons. The only option we had was to have the mussels in red sauce or white sauce, and the red or white wine in carafes intermittently placed along the tables. Everyone paid the same price and it was all you can eat. The roving musicians only added to the ambiance, gathering every half hour at the back of the dining hall to play Italian-American favorites at quite the volume. When our mouths weren't full with the most delicious Italian delicacies, we were singing along. When was the last time I could honestly say that I had so much fun in so little time with so many strangers?

Marc couldn't have been more of a gentleman. When he wasn't praising his newfound love, mainly me, he was speaking in Italian to some of the old men and women, who were obviously regulars. To top it all off, Marc joined the band to sing everyone's favorite, "That's Amore," with great zest and precision. Although I thought we'd revisit this place a number of times in the next couple of weeks, we never went back. I even suggested during the six-week courtship that we return to Celeste's. His reticence not only regarding Celeste's but also any other quaint and romantic restaurant disturbed me. It was then that I realized Celeste's was only the ground floor regarding impressing me with his dining repertoire. Two nights later we ate at Chez Nous Bien (a five-star restaurant near Gramercy Park), and I realized each time we dined, it was one step better than the last. What was next—dinner in Paris?

Marc even took me shopping between dinner dates and insisted on treating me to some of the nicest dinner wear I had ever owned. Most men are oblivious to what women wear. I discovered that another oddity that he possessed was his matching-outfit purchases. He always wanted us to match our attire, including our accessories.

Before I knew it, it was Thanksgiving and I had a four-day weekend coming. Trudging through another pre-Thanksgiving week of handprint turkeys and Native American and Pilgrim pageants, I was ready for a fun four-day furlough. Thanksgiving dinner was to be spent with my family; however, the morning was devoted to the Macy's Thanksgiving Day Parade. Charlene, my parade pal, called in the double-date ticket. Charlene and her husband Jared were to meet me at my apartment at 8:30 AM. We were going to take our two-avenue jaunt to meet Marc at Penn Station at 9:00 AM. Then we would make our way to the parade. In low-keyed fashion, the three of us meandered to Madison Square Garden. In a matter of minutes, Marc appeared, dressed to the nines. I couldn't understand why he was so overdressed, and questioned him about it. He answered, "I need to be, and later you'll find out why." This made me mildly concerned. Marc's flair for mystery was always lighthearted and amusing, but this time his face showed a sense of seriousness I hadn't recognized before. When I looked at Charlene, who overheard our conversation, she smiled and rolled her eyes. At that point I thought it was more than appropriate to introduce both my friends to Marc, who offered a polite handshake and small talk with both. Even the way Marc held my arm was strange. Something was different about him, and I couldn't put my finger on it.

We took the A, C, E line up to Columbus Circle to get to our planned viewing spot. But after exiting the subway and walking several blocks down along Broadway, he insisted on turning east down 57th Street and continuing for several blocks. When I asked him why we were passing the area in which we planned to watch the parade, he whispered, "You'll see." It was then that Charlene alerted me that the parade is in the other direction. I shrugged my shoulders and raised my eyebrows in complete confusion and kept walking as Marc hastily pulled me along. The street sign read 57th Street and 5th Avenue, the corner of Tiffany's & Company.

He stopped cold and turned around and said, "This is as good a place as any."

"I beg your pardon, but Charlene has friends reserving a spot for us at Broadway and 57th," I said.

"Does she have one of these?" Marc asked, producing a small box.

His Cheshire grin and boyish charm compelled me forward to see what was inside the box. I honestly hoped it wasn't what I thought it was, but it was. It was the most gaudy, obtrusive, obscene diamond engagement ring I had ever seen in my life. There was no proportion or balance to the setting. It appeared to be at least ten carats! Obviously, one of his jewelers had put this together for him in haste.

"You won't find one of these in there," Marc proclaimed while pointing to the corner window of Tiffany's. "Damn right," I thought to myself. Tiffany's wouldn't carry anything as tasteless as that. What was I to say? What was I to do? I stole a glance at Charlene, who pretended not to be listening or watching the embarrassing moment.

I whispered, "I can't, Marc. We've only been seeing each other for six weeks." He stood without talking. I continued and lied, "It's beautiful! I just can't, but thank you."

"Will you at least think about it?" Marc questioned.

"Sure, let's just enjoy the parade. Thanks again. It was very thoughtful."

Charlene immediately felt my embarrassment and confusion and yelped, "We're going to be late, and we have to go three avenue blocks in two minutes, not to miss the start of the parade."

Now I was pulling him like a deflated balloon. As I thought of the word balloon, I saw the huge Macy's turkey making its way down Broadway and heard Charlene yell, "It started, it started!" For the remainder of the day, Marc said only ten words to me. Nevertheless, Charlene, Jared, and I had a great time at the parade, pointing, laughing, and taking photos for the entire duration.

It was then time to make the trip out to Long Island to my parents' house for Thanksgiving dinner. Marc said he wasn't feeling well and would accompany me only if I insisted. I told him to go home and get rest. I added that we'd talk tomorrow. The ride in Charlene and Jared's SUV was a comfortable one. Charlene's inspiration and "attagirl" attitude made me feel good about my decision regarding Marc's proposal. Even Jared agreed that six weeks was way too soon to propose and added that it was also inappropriate and presumptuous of Marc on all fronts. Believe it or not, I didn't miss Marc at all at my parents' house, and no one asked where he was. Ironically, my brother John was also there alone and we had time to catch up on literary topics. I told him about *Breakfast at Tiffany's* and the bizarre incident that I just endured hours before, and he laughed and stated simply, "Sometimes life imitates art, Trish." I smiled and shook my head and made a beeline for another helping of stuffing.

During the next two weeks, I heard nothing from Marc. As a matter of fact, it was December 14 when he contacted me, strangely enough, via e-mail. The message said: "If you're interested, my holiday office party is on December 21, and there are people I'd like you to meet. I reluctantly agreed, but told him that the week before Christmas was busy for me. I would meet him at the party. I got the address and the time and the attire, which was surprisingly formal. December 21 came, and I found myself on Park Avenue at a hotel bar waiting for Marc. It didn't strike me at first, but soon I realized that I was the only female there. He told me 8:00, and by 8:35, I was ready to leave. Although the men in the bar all seemed professional, they were casually dressed, which made me feel silly in a gown. Maybe this wasn't where the party was. I looked around again and there wasn't another woman in sight. It looked like a yuppie bachelor party.

As I made my way toward the door, Marc came through it. He had on a sweater, jeans, and loafers.

"Why are you dressed like that?" I asked him.

"Like what?" he snapped.

"Like that," I said pointedly. "You said it was formal."

"Oh, I meant casual."

"Where's the party?" I inquired.

"You're in it," he snickered.

"Fellas, I want you to meet someone." I heard him laugh as he was walking away.

I was hot, red hot, with anger. Between my red face and my pale blue gown, I felt like a human Orange Bowl parade float on New Year's Day. That float was not going to be paraded for that jackass any longer. Even with three-inch heels, I made it out of that bar faster than I thought my legs could carry me. My nostrils never stopped flaring until I was in a cab heading home. To this day I don't know if I imagined it, or heard the men laughing in unison. But it doesn't matter. I wouldn't have anything to do with that joker again.

12

If Something Smells Fishy, It Usually Is

April 2000

The following three months were some of the coldest winter months I had ever experienced. Between the freezing temperatures and frequent snowstorms, I rarely went out at night. I found myself reading voraciously while sporting my flannel nightgown. I couldn't stop! Reading was addictive, especially during the winter months. I remember one particular week in February, just after my birthday, when I was in the middle of three different novels: one romance, one detective, and one British classic. I finally found out what a pip was, other than one of Gladys Knight's singers. Charles Dickens was right; *Great Expectations* was his best novel. I knew I was getting bad when I borrowed Melville's *Moby Dick* from the public library. But I'm glad I did because what a whale of a tale I found myself in, only five weeks later. Captain Ahab couldn't have prepared me any better.

April of 2000 was much drier than the previous year. It was so dry that the Easter plants looked puny and unhealthy. For the first time in years I didn't buy any and felt bad as a result. My cheesy silk flowers would have to hold me over till summer. Late one evening, toward the end of April, I accidentally stumbled upon the Discovery Channel. The show devoted itself to deep-sea fishing, namely marlin, swordfish, and tuna. I normally don't watch this sort of thing, yet found myself enthralled. It kept reminding me of Ishmael's faithful journey in *Moby*

Dick. The sheer strength of these great fish was outstanding. Not only did the fight of these fish fascinate me, but also the deep determination of the fishermen was interesting.

It was at that time I received an e-mail from New Rochelle. The sender was Jay, an avid fly fisherman. I laughed at the coincidence, for it was only weeks ago that I struggled through the nearly 600 pages of *Moby Dick*, and now I had a fisherman on the line myself. He stated in his note that he enjoyed fishing in general, fly-fishing in particular, and was currently making a living from it. "Hmm, a rugged outdoorsman," I thought, which reminded me of my childhood days of watching *Grizzly Adams* on television. My mind's eye saw a muscular, six foot tall, bearded, adventurous daredevil who knew the aquatic life. Maybe this was just what I needed—a break from the hustle and bustle of the city streets and the overdressed "glitter boys" who were unsuccessfully trying to impress me.

I responded to Jay's e-mail and requested a recent photo. He sent me what appeared to be a photo of a face behind a counter in a bait shop—a counter full of fishing paraphernalia and crab cages. To make matters worse, he had a baseball cap on, which appeared to have a variety of hooks hanging from the sides of the hat. The picture was obscured by all the crap on the counter, and the image quality was poor. I decided to decline.

Now that I think of it, he was as relentless as Ahab himself, yet unfortunately I was his great white whale. Each time he contacted me, he described himself differently. One time he described himself as five foot eleven inches with brown hair and blue eyes. Another time he described himself as funny and cuddly. I should have realized that "cuddly" is also a euphemism for someone who is overweight. I didn't mind a few extra pounds, for I was over the normal weight for my height, but I didn't find that we had much in common from reading his note, so I didn't respond. After two more e-mails from Jay, imploring me to give him a chance, I thought a phone call couldn't hurt. After speaking with him for more than an hour, he had me in stitches. So we arranged a date for a few days later.

He picked a seafood restaurant in the South Street Seaport—how apropos. I took a cab to Harbour Lights (a renowned seafood restaurant in the district). It had been some time since I had been down to South Street. Ironically, in the previous ten years I think I had been to Fisherman's Wharf in San Francisco more often. It was good to be back. Although heavily laden with tourists and the fish industry itself, I enjoyed the great ships and shops of the district.

I was so taken with the surroundings that I had not noticed the cabdriver had stopped his cab. "Harbour Lights, ma'am. We're here."

"Oh," I awoke from my daydream. "How much do I owe you?"

"That will be twelve dollars, "he responded.

As I attempted to exit my cab, I was shocked at what I saw: the most enormous, obnoxious, big-wheeled, pickup truck sat on the cobblestone sidewalk outside the restaurant. Along the side of the front fender, driver's door, and back bed fender, spelled the letters JAY—, PROFESSIONAL FLY FISHERMAN. "Oh my God," I said to myself. "That must be him!"

I couldn't believe it. How tacky (no pun intended). As I walked closer, I noticed that Jay was still in the pickup truck. He spotted me and began waving wildly. He motioned me over and I reticently walked up to the driver's side. The vision of what I saw next is unfortunately etched forever in my mind. I wasn't sure which was worse: the size of his huge beer belly behind the steering wheel or the dashboard that was laden with hundreds of colorful flies adhered with Velcro. Realizing my astonishment, he proceeded to tell me that not only were these examples his finest craftsmanship, but his truck also doubled as his showroom. He even referred me to his Web site, where he sells custom-made flies for fly fisherman all over the world. At this point, something smelled fishy (this time pun intended)! For obvious reasons, the date took a plunge. There was no chemistry, along with the lunacy of it all, and I began writing about the experience as soon as I got in a cab to go home. Once home, I looked up the Web site to see if it was just a big joke. To my surprise, it really existed.

13

If It Looks Too Good to Be True, It Usually Is

June 2000

No sooner did I let the big fish get away, than I decided to deviate from the normal Internet dating site that I had been using. I posted a profile on a Christian singles site. With my mom being a devout Catholic, I thought maybe it would be better to follow her advice. I assumed that most of these men would be family oriented, religious, and spiritual, and they would be the least likely to have a sexual perversion of some kind. I am a little less naive today than I was back then.

By mid-June I had received no e-mails worth mentioning. Joe, on the other hand, drew my attention. His e-mail portrayed him as a family oriented, fun-loving, outgoing guy. He stated that he prayed the rosary daily. Other than his excessive praying, I sensed a down-to-earth, regular guy. As a rule, I normally don't entertain potential dates outside a fifty-mile radius (due to my past perilous experiences). Mapquest claims that Anaheim is 3,100 miles away. I was never good in math in high school; however, that's far more than fifty miles! Duh! Nevertheless, Joe's piercing blue eyes and flaxen hair lured me (no pun intended).

Three weeks later, after we had spoken on the phone and exchanged photos, Joe flew east for a weekend visit. He was half Irish, half Mexican, and stood five foot ten inches. As a college-educated private investigator, Joe's expertise was in insurance fraud. Since insurance fraud is among the top ten felonious activities in this country, I thought this was an admirable vocation. He asked if it would be acceptable to fly to New York, as he had just solved a big case. He claimed he needed some time to clear his head, since the case took nearly two months to crack, and a weekend away from it all would be advantageous. In addition, he wanted to meet me as soon as possible.

While driving to Newark International Airport, I wondered if this could be the one. I wondered if he'd be attracted to me. Everything looked great! What could go wrong?

The weekend went very well. I asked what his preferences were, and before I could finish the question, he blurted, "The Bronx Zoo…and also the Botanical Gardens, of course!" I thought to myself, "That's funny. I haven't been to the Bronx Zoo since I was a child, and I can't remember ever visiting the Botanical Gardens."

The weekend proceeded as planned: a Broadway show (I wanted to see *Phantom*, but he urged *Cats*, and *Cats* it was), dinner at the renowned Smith & Wollensky Steak House, and a walk through Central Park. His attention was drawn to the horse-pulled carriages.

"Is this just on the weekends or…?"

"No, Joe," I interrupted. "This is 24/7, twelve months a year—weather permitting, of course."

After his fascination with this phenomenon, our conversation steered itself toward more important things. He offered that his father had been a well-known horse veterinarian, licensed in the states of California and New Mexico. After ten minutes of his father's veterinarian accomplishments, I finally asked him about the other members of his family. Joe was no less passionate. He proceeded to praise his mother for her daily devotion to St. Francis of Assisi, the great protector of animals. When it came to his oldest sister, Marion, he couldn't stop. After fifteen minutes of Marion adulation, I asked him about his other five siblings. Although warm and genial, his descriptions were nothing like those of his mother and Marion. It was clear to me that the maternal instinct in this family was its guiding light. The only problem I sensed was that when he spoke of his father, he looked down at his shoes. Yet when he spoke of his mother and sister, we were eye-to-eye. When I asked him if both parents were still alive, his demeanor changed, and to this day, I can't determine whether it was from sadness or aloofness. However, it certainly wasn't sadness when he spoke of his father's departure. Regardless, I knew not to press on in that area and questioned him instead about his home life. Once again, his eyes danced with elation. For more than twenty minutes he described his family's ranch from one end to the other. Everything from the farm hands to the little triangle his mother insisted on ringing every night at seven o'clock for dinner. He literally could have talked for hours about the years he spent on that ranch, but before we knew it we were standing in front of the Museum of Natural History, clear across Central Park. He must have sensed my agitation because he squeezed my hand and asked what was wrong. I told him that we had walked the equivalent of thirty blocks (the diagonal distance of Central Park), and it was two o'clock in the morning!

At that point he asked, "Is that bad?"

I said, "No, time flies when you're having fun."

He immediately responded with, "What's next?"

"A cab ride back to my apartment and then to your hotel," I replied.

I readied myself for his deflation, for he was soaring like a parade balloon. But it never came. He was as positive about the cab ride to his hotel room as he was about the ranch, family outings, and even the periodic religious retreats they held in their own home. My mother's prayers were being answered, I thought.

Sunday's brunch was as good as Saturday's dinner. He ate the way a true farmhand would—everything in sight. I honestly thought he would eat the tablecloth as well, until I reminded him that his flight was at two thirty that afternoon out of Macarthur Airport on Long Island, not Newark, where he had arrived. Although Long Island at the time was in a middle of a building boom, there were enough horse farms along the way at which Joe could marvel. He was like a kid in a candy store. He couldn't have been happier. There was something about those horses that intrigued him.

As promised, I was aboard a California-bound plane six days later. It was truly time for a California vacation. It had been quite a while since my last getaway. I met his family. They were all wonderful and hospitable. Although Joe and I had met in New York City only days before, I debated whether this was love or just extreme infatuation. It didn't matter which, as I looked around at the most beautiful scenery of Southern California (all owned by Joe's family). I enjoyed myself to the max. One problem, though, was that all the mother and sisters could speak about were religious matters. Raised a strict Catholic myself, I endured their conversation as best I could. However, when I sensed they were testing my faith with the most inane, dogmatic, questions about principles, I tolerated it no further. I politely excused myself and began my long arduous search for Joe. Entering one of the four chicken coops on the ranch, (the only lighted one), I must have startled him because he nearly jumped out of his skin.

"How many chickens do you have to feed on this ranch?" I said, trying to calm him.

"Less than half of what we had in our heyday," he demurely answered.

"Where are the horses?" I asked.

"Oh, that's another thing. When my father died, they were no longer an issue. There's only Leo, the burro to keep these chickens in line."

As he said this, he pointed to the most ancient long-eared animal I have ever seen. This donkey must have been seventy years old, if he was a day. I didn't have the heart to ask him about the burro, when I sensed his somber mood over the horse issue. This time I was the one to ask the question "what's next?"

"Let me finish this row. I'll clean up, and then I'll show you my humble abode."

On the way to his apartment complex, I asked him what was planned for the following day. Again, before I could finish the question, his answer was, "The zoo, of course."

"What zoo are you referring to?" I inquired.

"The Los Angeles Zoo," he snapped.

Realizing that it was only a twenty-five-mile ride from Anaheim, I felt comfortable. Like a true gentleman, he dropped me off at my motel first. He told me that he would give me the cook's tour of his apartment the following afternoon. After a nice day at the zoo and a quaint lunch at a local restaurant, I found myself back at Joe's apartment with more questions than answers. His mood changed dramatically the moment the key turned in the door of his apartment.

What met me first was a bulletin board to the left of the kitchen doorway. Pinned to that board were at least a dozen snapshots of perpetrators of various crimes sought by the local police. Adjacent to the bulletin board was a chalkboard, which was a virtual timetable or schedule for the comings and goings of these perps. On the dining room wall was an enormous area map of Southern California and western Arizona. Protruding from the map was a myriad of colored flagged pins apparently indicating where these perpetrators lived and worked. On the dining room table were several computers, printers, and fax machines, all seemingly in operation. On both the coffee table and end tables were mountains of manila folders, which were obviously files that Joe was either working on or had finished. Adorning each wall of the three rooms I could see, were photographs and paintings of racehorses past and present. Even the curtains of the living room had images of cowboys chasing Indians on fast-moving horses. Before I could pummel Joe with questions about the odd indoor scene, I asked him where the bathroom was. It was as if I woke him from a slumber. He looked at me as if he didn't know who I was.

"Oh, I am sorry, Trish. I just picked up an important fax from the Anaheim Police Department."

"That's OK, Joe. You look like a busy man."

"It's down the hall, two doors to your right," he concluded.

What I experienced next was the second most frightening element of the trip. Instinctively I looked into the first room on the right, which was the guest bedroom. In the room were a daybed, dresser, and night table. However, on every square foot of the room, including the walls, appeared statues, paintings, and pictures of the Sacred Heart, Mary, saints, and angels. I slowed my pace and glanced nonchalantly into the room on the left. In that room, it seemed as if I was looking at a religious article supermarket; life-sized statues of holy entities filled the room. Even the headboard was carved with an image of the Last Supper. This morbidly reminded me of the estate in England. Regardless, obsession is obsession, and I was always taught that obsession is wrong.

My bladder couldn't hold out another second. As I opened the bathroom door, I saw what appeared to be a shrine on top of the toilet and sink. Smaller statues, rosary beads, and votive candles crowded the lavatory. On the walls were more photographs of various horses. Even the shower curtain had images of the Kentucky Derby. Uncomfortably relieving my bladder's tension, and trying to put these images out of my mind, I instinctively looked to the sink. What pushed me over the top were the little hand soaps shaped like horses in one dish and soaps shaped like angels in the other. Now I was genuinely concerned.

As I exited the bathroom and had to walk down what seemed to be the longest hallway, I refused to look in either room. I arrived in the living room and called Joe's name. No answer. I continued into the dining room and kitchen, but there was still no answer. "That's odd," I thought. "He was here only a few moments ago. Where could he be?" It was then I saw the piece of computer paper floating in midair in the kitchen. I thought, "This is too spooky." However, I had to determine what I thought I just saw. The paper wasn't floating at all; it was attached to the cord that controlled the overhead fan and light. Handwritten on the paper were the following words: "Sorry Trish, had to leave quickly. Hot tip on a perp. Be back within the hour. Love, Joe." This increased my anxiety, because then I had to sit for at least sixty minutes in an apartment that resembled a bizarre chapel or perhaps a tack room in a jockey's hangout.

What was I to do for an hour or more? The next discovery was as bizarre as the others. There was no television or even radio in the entire apartment, just the three computers. I went to the door and looked out at a parking lot. Retreating back, I sat at the dining room table. My eyes became fixed on the closed laptop at the far end of the table. Since the battery on my cell phone was running dangerously low, I decided to contact my good friend Greg (via e-mail) and ask him what I should do under these circumstances. I didn't think Joe would mind. This laptop looked as if it was used for personal business, not like the other two, which looked more official.

When I opened up the lid, I wasn't surprised to see one of the greatest racehorses on his screensaver. Man O'War was proudly posing for a twenties black-and-white photograph, alongside his jockey and owner. Since Joe never logged off or shut down, the computer was still running. Innocently, I clicked on the browser icon to sign on to my e-mail account. This could fill up some idle time while I waited for Joe. After all, I do watch too much television and listen to too much music.

Before I could compose an e-mail to Greg, I was inundated with many pop-ups depicting what appeared to be animals mating. As I began to close each spam window, I couldn't believe my eyes! Perhaps I had seen too many pictures of horses in his apartment, and my eyes were deceiving me. Upon closer inspection, I realized that these weren't animals mating; these were animals and humans mating (is mating the right term here?). My curiosity took over, knowing these spam pop-ups only happen when one visits similar sites. I decided to do some investigating of my own.

To my disgust, as I clicked on the history icon, I encountered hundreds of thumbnails of movie and photo files that had the word animal in them. I randomly clicked on one of them, and it opened a bestiality movie of a woman getting it on with a Great Dane! I thought my eyes were playing tricks on me, so I clicked on the next one and found another woman with a horse. Gross! To think that we had been at the San Diego Zoo only a day before. What the hell had he been thinking? And even worse, his deceased father had been a well-known horse veterinarian. Not only would I have to worry about other women, but animals as well. This was more bizarre than I could have thought. Just then the front door handle began to turn, and thinking it was Joe, I rose and hastily made a beeline toward the door. At that moment I realized it was too late to log off and close the laptop. Much to my surprise it wasn't Joe at all, but Marion, his oldest sister.

"What's wrong, Trish? You looked like you saw a ghost," she said. Before I could answer, I saw her eyes move down the table to the open laptop and the chair left askew.

"Oh, I see." She added, "There's a perfectly good explanation."

"My phone battery was running low, and I needed to contact a friend to verify my ride home from the airport...."

"No need to explain yourself," Marion retorted.

As she finished her statement I noticed her somber mood. She sat and invited me to do the same. She began to tell a lurid tale of Joe's preoccupation with animals, stemming from their father's profession.

She told me that her mother had befriended a priest when her dad had developed cancer. The priest supposedly had healing powers. He spent time with the family in an effort to comfort them. At this point she revealed that Joe had been molested by the priest when he was younger. I asked her how old he was when this terrible thing happened, expecting to hear that he was a child. But instead, she replied that he was 19—it had happened only ten years prior! I was shocked! Could this be what had caused his imbalance? Then it came to me, as Marion continued to supply many details regarding the facts. I silently pieced the puzzle together. The combination of what Joe saw as a child, perhaps in his father's office, the ranch life of animal husbandry, and the molestation of an unstable young adult by a Catholic priest, all contributed to his perversion.

Marion continued her explanation while I retrieved my purse and sunglasses. I politely asked her to drop me off at my motel room and implored her not to reveal the nature of my departure. She agreed, and before long we were in the parking lot outside my room.

"I am sorry for all of this, Trish, but Joe is a good kid. Please remember him as such."

"Right now, Marion, I need to sort things out. I'm a little shaken," I responded.

"Take all the time you need. You appear to be a good kid yourself."

As she drove out of the parking lot, I felt an overwhelming sadness for that family. I realized at that point how fortunate it was to be "normal." The next morning came and went with a quick cab ride to the airport, surrounded by the beauty of Southern California. I had never been this far south in California before, and I absolutely loved the scenery. What a beautiful region of the country. Just then I had a bizarre thought. Actually it was more of a joke that I had heard when I was a kid but could never quite understand. It goes as follows: "Other than that, Mrs. Abraham Lincoln, how did you like the play?" I finally got that joke, which my father used to tell and my brothers used to laugh at.

14

Be Wary of Someone Too Eager to Travel a Great Distance Right Away

August 2000

I should have learned my lesson from chapter 3, where I traveled to England to visit Simon, but I didn't, and I gave the Christian Singles site another chance. Another zealot answered my ad. This time it was Ben from Dallas, Texas. Although average in height, build, and complexion, his smile spoke volumes. During the first conversation after our initial e-mail correspondence, he seemed to be interested in someone from the north. I told him that I was not interested in moving to Texas, nor any other southern state for that matter. I was New York bred and bound. He said that even though he owned a tree trimming business and was a certified arborist, he would be willing to go where the Lord took him. On the phone he sounded personable and upbeat. It bothered me that he was already willing to sacrifice a business and career and move north before even meeting me. That spelled desperation to me.

With that in mind, I dug as deeply as I could with my questions to uncover the crack in his foundation. If I was successful, I would politely dismiss myself from the situation and move on. The more I dug, the less I found. He seemed to have answers for everything, most of which were logical and sound. His kind personality and phone presence warmed my heart. After several of these conversations over the span of two weeks, I decided to invite him to New York for a weekend. He jumped at the chance. "Why wait until next weekend, why not tomorrow?" he exclaimed.

Tomorrow? That was too eager for me. What is wrong with these guys who are willing to drop everything and fly 1,500 miles or more to be with someone they have never met? Now I truly understand why they call some southwestern cowboys *desperados*. I told him that tomorrow was no good, nor was the rest of the week for that matter. I got this strange mental image of three cowpokes standing up and spilling tin cups of coffee to put out their campfire. His silence on the phone was deafening.

"Are you still there, Ben?" I urged.

"Call me 'Heck,' will you Trish?"

"Heck," I thought to myself. "I feel like I am in an episode of *Bonanza*, waiting for Little Joe and Hoss to walk in and lecture me on why I should take Heck up on his offer."

"How do you spell that, Ben? I asked.

"Heck, H-e-c-k, like 'oh Heck,'" he responded.

Now I was really in it! Second thoughts bombarded me. How can I get myself the *heck* out of this one? I finally told him that the following weekend would be better. This delay would allow me some time to think of an excuse not to go through with it.

Less than ten minutes later, the phone rang again. Heck was on the other line proclaiming that he had booked a flight over the Internet for $265 to New York, eight days away.

Eight days flew by, and my anticipation was practically nonexistent. I begrudgingly made it through Friday night rush hour traffic to JFK airport and waited at the gate for Heck to arrive. As I tried to imagine how this experience could turn out positively, Heck walked off the plane with a freaking cowboy hat, cowboy boots, faded denim jeans, and a red bandana. The only things missing were a holster and a piece of wheat between his teeth. He looked as if he stepped off the soundstage for an episode of *Gunsmoke*.

As I was driving him from the airport to his hotel, I decided to cut right to the chase. After a long-winded discussion about three saints, I finally asked him if he engaged in any online activity that he wasn't proud of (since that had been a real deal-killer in the past for me). He switched gears and told me that God allows him to view porn online as a physical outlet to prepare him for the sacrament of marriage. He claimed that God spoke to him often and that God had actually guided him and had given him signs to meet me. He even confided to me that only a few years before, at the age of thirty, he would frequent topless bars to persuade the dancers to turn to God. One night he brought a dancer home, and she took advantage of him and stole his virginity. What a crock of shit! At that point, I wanted to drop the freak off by the side of the road at Sheep's Head Bay on the Belt Parkway! But no, I'd gotten myself stuck in this mess. I had to deal with him. My mind was racing, so I planned what chores needed to be done that weekend so that the weekend would not be a total waste.

We arrived in New York City and went to dinner at a diner. I ordered a cheeseburger and fries, and he sat there and lectured me on how fattening and unhealthy my food was. At this point I truly felt ashamed of my food choices, but I defensively responded, "I don't care. If I want a damn burger, I'll have it." It was then that I found out that he wasn't only a religious fanatic, but also a health nut too. He wasn't happy. He continued to badger me about the ill effects of eating meat. He claimed that in the last stages of becoming certified as an arborist he had learned a lot about the world of vegetarianism. He said that he had firmly converted himself and his workers.

He should have asked me to call him Hick, instead of Heck, for that's truly what he morphed into as the hours transpired. He not only lectured me, but included everyone in the restaurant, and the city of New York for our unhealthy eating habits and meat-eating ways. He continued what seemed to be a sermon at that point, about how God gave us one body and it was not up to us to destroy it with toxic foods. He said he would pray to the archangel Gabriel for my forgiveness, as if Gabriel had nothing more to do than check souls at the gate of heaven (as far as Heck was concerned, he checked their waistlines as well).

I now knew the first order of business would be to remove my profile from the Christian singles site. I only wished that I could discover a better way to find a life partner. My mind was made up; I couldn't take another minute, let alone two more days, of this crap.

In the middle of one of Heck's rants about the lack of serious concern for ecology in New York City by its residents, I purposefully dropped my knife on the plate to make a scene. The sound was twice as loud as I had thought it would be. Many of the diner patrons stopped their dinner conversations and stared at me. That was just what I had wanted.

"That's enough!" I yelled, "There's nothing wrong with me, these people, or the city of New York for that matter. This is our home. Why don't you take your cattleman's ass back to Dallas where you are obviously more comfortable and more needed? This city is full of transplants and we don't need another one. Do you hear that sound, Heck?"

"No, what?" Heck responded.

"That is the Lord calling you. You mentioned you would go wherever the Lord called you. I hear him calling you out of New York."

I abruptly jumped out of the booth and threw a twenty on the table and headed for the door. Luckily, as soon as I left the diner, a cab pulled up. I was home in less than ten minutes.

15

Don't Date Someone Who Has Never Been in a Relationship

December 2000

It was hard to believe that it was only a little more than a year ago that I was standing outside of Tiffany's, being proposed to by an overly ambitious Don Juan type. Where did those thirteen months go? Thanksgiving had come and gone, and Macy's had decorated its window a week early this year. "Great," I thought to myself, "another Christmas without a relationship." As a child I had loved Christmas, but as an adult this season wasn't as jolly. I guessed there would be little "Ho Ho Ho" this Christmas, too (or maybe not). "Regardless," I thought to myself, "this Christmas I am going to have a great time—with or without someone." Thank God for Internet shopping. I could find an outfit, new shoes, and even a nice coat for myself without enduring all of the Christmas hype and gaudy displays in the department stores, which only made me self-conscious about my singleness. No sooner did I sit down to begin my splurge, than the ever-familiar ring of those three words was heard: "You have mail." "Fantastic," I thought to myself. When I get in the shopping mode, that's all I want to do, and I don't like to be distracted. As I sat debating whether to ignore my e-mail, I noticed that my screen saver appeared and made my decision for me. The lonely little snowman melting in the noonday sun that I chose for my screen saver seemed lonelier now than a week ago. Even the little pool of melted snow around his base seemed wider. Damn, he looked depressed! I decided to postpone my shopping splurge for a few minutes and read my e-mail.

Mickey wrote only a few lines, stating that he was looking for a partner to enjoy the fun things in life, especially around the Christmas holidays. He stated that he was six foot two inches, and of Irish-German descent. His photo showed that he was attractive. He worked part-time at an Internet start-up company located in New York City and part-time as a caddie in Rockland County, where he lived. "Rockland," I thought to myself. "That's funny, I don't know if I have ever met anyone from Rockland County. How bad could this one be?"

I sent Mickey my phone number and he immediately called! He sounded mildly interesting, aside from his monotone delivery. Based on last year's mistakes with out-of-state men, I decided to stay closer to home and concentrate on the greater metropolitan area. I also liked the notion of cutting to the chase early for quick exit purposes. I began the interview process. I asked Mickey about his last relationship, how many long-term or short-term relationships he had had. His response was that he had never had a relationship. Up went the red flag! This surprised me because he had reached the age of forty without a commitment to a serious relationship. Will wonders never cease? I didn't think there were any forty-year-old virgins these days, or maybe I was being too presumptuous. I decided to give Mickey a try, due to his innocent divulgence of this very sensitive matter.

Each time we spoke on the phone, the conversation flowed better than the time before. I had asked him why he had never had a relationship, but he refused to answer and told me that he would discuss it when we met. Since he worked in the city and I lived there, we decided to meet for pizza at a neighborhood parlor close to Penn Station. If the date didn't pan out, it would be beneficial for both of us to be that close to Penn Station. He could easily hop on the 1, 2, or 3 train to Times Square at 42nd, then transfer to the S to Grand Central to Metro North to his park-and-ride at White Plains and proceed on to Rockland County, and it allowed me to make a quick getaway as well, since I lived only a few blocks away. If the date went well, we could enjoy the Christmas decorations in Macy's windows.

When we finally met, he looked like his photo, but appeared thinner. He seemed very nervous in the beginning, but after twenty minutes he became more comfortable. I was still curious as to why he had never had a relationship, so I asked him again. His response was that he had gone on many first dates, but was never pursued by any of his contacts, due to his drinking and excess weight. As a result of severe depression and low self-esteem, he decided to attend weekly AA meetings, where he had great success. Sober for seven years, Mickey exuded a great sense of accomplishment. "Seven years," I thought. "All those years without a drink or a relationship? I've had dry spells in the past, but this is unbelievable!" He said that he had lost weight and now felt great about himself. Most women would probably have left at that point in the date but I stayed, and the teacher in me gave him an "A" for honesty. He seemed lovable, but maybe life had just dealt him the wrong hand.

"This could be another *Miracle on 34th Street*," I laughed to myself. But maybe it was too early to decide. After a mutually good time, we both agreed that a movie would be in order, so we walked down the street to the Loews on 34th. We decided to see *Almost Famous*. After the second sex scene in the movie, I couldn't help but wonder about Mickey. I discreetly turned to him and whispered, "If you have never had a relationship, does that mean you are a virgin as well?" He told me that he would tell me later, if I promised not to judge him. Uh-oh, what had I gotten myself into now? The curiosity was eating me alive. There was at least another hour of the movie left, and my anxiety soared!

Finally the movie ended, credits rolled, and we exchanged small talk regarding the story line on the way out of the theatre. Once we arrived at the diner, I immediately ordered a piece of cake and a cup of tea, while he ordered nothing. I pleaded with him to order something. He said he wasn't hungry. "Then order something to drink," I said. Oops, wrong choice of words. He acquiesced by ordering a club soda. I realized then how hard it was for him, or anyone else, to remove an obsession such as alcoholism from one's life. Before I posed the question again, I assured Mickey that I had an open mind, as well as a diverse group of friends who were anything but ordinary.

"So tell me, Mickey, are you or are you not a virgin?" I inquired tactfully. I couldn't determine the cause of the redness he exhibited. Was it a blush of embarrassment or a sign of anger? Moments later it was clear to me that it was neither.

"I beg your pardon, Trisha, but you don't need to have a relationship to have sex," he retorted.

I felt foolish! He was right! Although quite forceful, Mickey remained polite and respectful throughout. I immediately apologized for my rudeness.

He responded with, "No need to apologize, Trish. There's nothing better than frankness on a first date. I admire that trait in you. Now let me be frank with you."

In the midst of his statement, I cut him off with one of my patented questions, "Don't tell me that you use the Internet for those encounters, do you?"

"As a matter of fact, I do, now that you asked."

Asked? Pried is more like it. I was actually prying into his personal life, and I had only known him for just a few hours. Who was I to do that? But then again, this was my life and I didn't want to get involved with anyone without a normal sense of control regarding his sexual impulses. Mickey continued. It was downright shocking what he revealed in the next few minutes. He told me that he had been meeting with prostitutes (high-end call girls, as he referred to them) over the past seven "dry" years. He admitted that at times these encounters were weekly and that the highest-end whore was upwards of $500. I am glad that he didn't tell me what he paid for the low-end ladies. Without pause, he detailed the different Web sites he had done business with. The only drawback seemed to be the expenses he had (not for the hos, but for the "ho"-tel rooms, due to the fact that he lived with his parents). His demeanor never wavered. It was almost as if he was proud of his accomplishments (sexual conquests is what I called them). I decided to let Mickey talk until he was finished rather than deliver my own philosophy regarding the issue. The last thing I remember him saying was that he was going to treat himself to a high-class call girl this Christmas if this date doesn't work out. I thought to myself, "Well then, make your call, boy, because this isn't going anywhere." Although there weren't any Ho Ho Hos in my Christmas that year, I'm sure Mickey had a few of his own.

16

Pay Attention to Red Flags

December 2000

Only a few weeks later, the week of Christmas, I ironically received an interesting e-mail from Jamie, a thirty-five-year-old attorney from Stamford, Connecticut. I say ironically because during the week of Christmas, Internet dating reaches its nadir. By that time of the year, most people have either found someone to share the holiday spirit with, or are preoccupied with their family responsibilities. Jamie, however, persisted throughout the week. After four e-mails and attachments, I finally wrote back. He had mentioned his recent separation in the previous e-mail and I became a bit gun-shy. Another steadfast rule of mine was to not date married men under any circumstances, separated or otherwise. That was only one of the four red flags that appeared regarding Jamie. But feeling festive, I agreed to meet him for a quick cup of coffee at a nearby coffee shop. That week's calendar was filled with obligations, so coffee was the best I could offer. He surprisingly agreed.

What's the worst that could happen? A new friend? I didn't realize at that point that my dance card was so full. Only when I was standing in Lord & Taylor did I realize that my list of friends to buy presents for was the length of my forearm. It may sound cruel, but I had no time for more acquaintances. Nevertheless, our coffee date went well (all fifty-three minutes of it), and we decided to keep in touch. He said it was just as well, since he hadn't begun his shopping yet. He would take advantage of being in the middle of the city, and, with any luck, he would conquer his shopping list. We bid farewell, and I went about planning my annual Christmas party for my friends. Only two days left. I thought he wouldn't call until after the holidays were over, but, much to my surprise, he called the next day. I thought it might be an attempt on his part to thank me and wish me happy holidays, but no, he wanted to get together the following evening. I told him that I couldn't make it, that I was having my annual gathering. His response was pushy. "Maybe we can kill two birds with one stone. Maybe you can invite me to your party and I can help you with the serving." It was then that I found out he had worked at a catering company to put himself through law school. Good naturedly, I agreed.

This turned out to be one of my greatest mistakes. Even as a child I brought home stray cats all too often. It just so happened that Jamie was involved in a major litigation that would, with any luck, end by December 23rd. The trials were taking place in New York City, and he would be free a few days before Christmas Eve. I was in the middle of baking cookies for a holiday party when my tree stand broke, scattering the tree and its decorations in the middle of my studio apartment. I tried desperately to upright the tree, but to no avail. Just then my cell phone rang. It was Jamie wanting to know what he could bring to the party. I told him a tree stand would be nice, as I nearly cried into the phone.

"You're joking," Jamie replied.

Choking back the tears, I exclaimed, "No, I'm not. It's late, and I have no time to get another one."

"Relax, I will take care of everything," he replied.

And that's just what he did. He showed up with two bottles of champagne, a box of cannoli, and the tree stand. He was adorably dressed in a red and green holiday sweater. He was a lifesaver. Not only did he fix the tree and help me serve throughout, he had everyone in tears of laughter with his dry sense of humor. Even my best friend, Anne, who is normally very depressed about being single during the holiday season, was in the best of spirits. Other than his high-pitched feminine-sounding voice and nervous twitch tugging on his right earlobe, I found him quite charming.

The following day Anne called me to thank me for the great evening at my party. I was about to use this as an opportunity to ask her what she thought about Jamie. No sooner did I get the words out of my mouth, than Anne told me that her initial impression was extremely positive. She thought that Jamie could be a prime example of the new "metrosexual"—a straight man who is in touch with his feminine side. She expressed that during the evening she had spent a fair bit of time talking with him. As Anne spoke about her work in the fashion industry, Jamie shared his knowledge regarding a variety of fabrics and an in-depth knowledge of design.

"What man knows what taffeta is?" Anne blurted.

"I know Jamie was married before, so perhaps his wife wore taffeta all the time," I joked.

"Oh, that's right. Come to think of it, Jamie mentioned that his soon-to-be-ex-wife owns a small boutique in Greenwich," Anne retorted.

"That explains his great attention to detail. It's a nice change to find a straight guy with fashion sense," I added.

"Do you think this could be serious?" Anne questioned.

"He's not only handsome, stylish, and funny, but intelligent as well," I giddily exclaimed.

Noticing my fondness for Jamie, Anne's last words rang over and over in my mind: "Although he appears wonderful on the surface, you know that you're a romantic, Trish. Don't let the magic of Christmas cloud your judgment."

During the following week, Jamie and I talked for several hours on the phone. He wanted to return the favor and did, so I found myself agreeing to his invitation to a New Year's Eve party being held at his home in Stamford. He shared this house with his brother and mother. This was another red flag. I was definitely out of my environment. Although the house looked old and somewhat stately from the road, it was overgrown with what appeared to be ancient trees, bushes, and ivy. Even the driveway looked decrepit and unkempt. What soothed my anxiety were the many cars in the long driveway leading to the house.

I decided to park my car at the bottom of the driveway, with the nose of the car facing the street. What I saw when I walked through the door reminded me of the ancient house from the old sitcom *The Munsters*. Instead of a fire-breathing dragon coming out of the staircase, the staircase was covered with cats. I could hear voices coming from the back of the house. I decided to join the party with Jamie. There were a few close family friends in an enormous great room that jutted out into the woods behind the house. He introduced me to his brother, Larry, who appeared somber and unmoved. It was only then that I realized my third mistake (red flag). During our initial conversation, Larry insisted on discussing his present infantile fetish involving diapers, pacifiers, and teething toys. It was apparent to me that Larry had severe emotional issues. At first I thought he was joking, but I turned to Jamie when Larry was in the bathroom and asked, "Is he for real?" Jamie said that he took after his mother, who is a paranoid schizophrenic restricted to her room upstairs on the third floor of the house. You would think this would be another red flag for me, but it actually intrigued me. I felt sorry for Jamie for having had such an unstable childhood. The house was the embodiment of a past turbulent life. I inquired whether his father was in the picture and what he was doing. Jamie explained that his dad, a psychiatrist, had left his mother and family for another woman and was living with her and her children in Costa Rica.

I laid it out on the table with more than a little sarcasm: "Online dating has given me the fortunate opportunity to meet myriad potential partners, such as: a foot fetish fellow, a sadistic psychiatrist, a religious fiend into bestiality, and a guy who frequents prostitutes that he orders online like you would order CDs, to name a few. Do me a huge favor: If you have anything that you are, or were, into, like these guys, please don't call me again." Jamie then looked me right in the eye and said, "I've never even looked at a *Playboy* magazine. My wife and I finally just fell out of love, and she abandoned me. I subsequently moved back into my childhood home to take care of my brother and mother." I felt sorry for him, just a lonely lost soul searching for love. I told him I felt the roads might ice up due to the cold temperatures, so he walked me to my car at the bottom of the driveway. The entire ride home was nothing short of disturbing. I don't know if it was the house, the brother, the mysterious mother upstairs (like the woman in *Jane Eyre*) or just the remoteness of everything. Nonetheless, I got home safely and slept like a baby (pun intended).

At this point, I was highly doubtful that Jamie and I would have a future together, but I was willing to leave the lines of communication open. Never did I think those lines of communication would cross so quickly. It was 10:00 AM New Year's Day, and I decided to take the tree down. No sooner did I package one box of ornaments, than the phone rang. Jamie was on his way down from Stamford to Manhattan. I had, in my haste to leave, inadvertently left my sweater behind and hadn't even realized it. Within a few minutes, the doorman buzzed to alert me that Jamie was in the lobby.

I said, "Send him right up, Ralph. Happy New Year to you and yours."

"Happy New Year to you, Trish, and thank you for your thoughtful gift."

I held the door waiting for Jamie as he exited the elevator with a giant smile on his face. With a peck on his cheek, I looked down and noticed he was wearing my sweater! Why in the hell would he be wearing my sweater? "He's so goofy," I thought.

"I think that color suits you," I chuckled.

"You really think so?" Jamie retorted.

"You were right about the snow; we lost power up in Connecticut. Is there any way that I can borrow your computer for a few minutes? I need to check on the progress of the trial with the firm."

"Of course, but I promised Greg that I would stop by for cappuccino at 11:00 AM. Can you manage it on your own?"

"Where does Greg live?" Jamie asked.

"Two doors down," I responded.

"Two buildings down?" he asked.

"No, two apartments down," I replied.

After I returned from Greg's apartment, as Jamie was using the bathroom, I checked my e-mail. As I was reading my e-mails, a slew of porn pop-ups took over my monitor. I then proceeded to check the history to see why this was happening. As it turned out, Jamie had not been working on his trial. He was viewing transsexual pornography! I became irate. I interrogated him, and he became angrier and angrier. I even went so far as asking, "Do you want to be a woman?" He said, "No," and then called me a few choice words and left abruptly.

It wasn't until five months later that I got a call from Jamie again. My first instinct was to hang up. But since we had unfinished business, I decided to hear him out and listen to what he had to say. He expressed that I had been the only person who had the potential to truly understand him. After an hour of a heart-wrenching conversation, I found out that over the past five months he had embarked on pursuing a gender change. He had begun hormone therapy as well as facial plastic surgery. He confided that, although he really wanted to be a woman, the reason he had answered my profile is that he admired the type of woman I was, and that he wanted to emulate me. I also found out that over the previous year, he had answered personal ads of transsexuals and transvestites, had cross-dressed in private, had gone to gay bars dressed as a woman complete with wig, makeup, padded girdle, high heels, fake nails, etc. He shared with me that he was going to therapy for gender dysphoria. At first I was pissed because he had misrepresented himself in a major way, but that passed, and I felt that I might want to help him.

My brain must have been on vacation, because there were several major red flags on this journey with Jamie. But as you know, people ignore red flags, and some people have the need to help others in a crisis. I will always wish Jamie well and hope he will be happy when he becomes a she for good.

17

Long Hair Doesn't Always Equal a GAP Model

February 2001

Out of the pan and into the fire? Maybe I should have waited, but in hot pursuit I retreated hastily to the dreadful dating Web site. To this point, the clean-cut collegiate look had failed me. Although I prefer that look, I was due for a change. Growing up in a household with three brothers who had pushed the limits of acceptability during the seventies (my oldest brother had waist-length hair), I had seen enough of the subculture that that decade yielded! I had made a pact with myself: my hair must be longer than my date's hair. However, short-haired "Internuts" had brought me nothing but confusion and aggravation for four years, so maybe it was time that *I* let my hair down.

Little did I know, it would turn out that I wasn't the one letting my hair down. Matt, a professional musician, had sent me a response. His picture showed a good-looking surfer type, with shoulder-length hair. Maybe this is just what I needed! A change of pace was in order! Since he appeared younger than I, I immediately went to the age box. Ironically, he had left it blank. "Good," I said to myself. Maybe the suspected age difference was what the doctor ordered. Until that point, I had been dating men much older than I. It might benefit me, I thought, to be in some control, even if the controlling factor was the age difference. After a decade of living downtown, I had had my fill of looking at the bohemian type. Then again, the male supermodels for the GAP and Tommy Hilfiger have curiously long hair! It was time to get over my fear of flowing follicles.

After a few e-mail exchanges, I realized that he was indeed younger than I. His taste in music and his obsession with motorcycles led me to believe he was at least four (maybe five) years my junior. That intrigued me. Let's face it; every woman at one time or another in her life has fantasized about a younger man. Perhaps I was having my turn. "Go for it," I thought to myself. So I made a date for the following Thursday for Matt to meet me in the lobby of my apartment building. I gave Ralph, my doorman, a leg up on the situation. After two or three sentences of fatherly advice, I assured Ralph that that kind of date was what I needed at that point in my life. With slight hesitancy, Ralph assented. He would buzz me the moment Matt showed up.

"Want me to give him the third degree, Trish?"

"Please, Ralph. The last thing I need now is a surrogate father. I could use a vigilant friend."

"As a father of two boys, I never had a daughter, and you're the closest thing to it!"

"You're a sweet man, Ralph."

"We don't want another one like Jamie," Ralph responded as he walked back to his post.

I felt the little three-pronged pitchfork sting my neck again. It had been a long time since that cartoonlike devil had warned me of an impending disaster. I waited for his counterpart, but the little angel never played a note of encouragement on her harp. "That's odd," I thought to myself. Nevertheless, I decided to go through with it. The sheer excitement alone attracted me.

Ralph was true to his word. At precisely 7:45 the following evening, his kindhearted voice followed the annoying buzz. "Your date's here. Don't rush," he yelled emphatically.

"What was that all about?" I said to myself. I grabbed my purse, coat, scarf, and hat, because it was twenty degrees (with a wind chill in the single digits) that night. "Don't rush," I thought to myself over and over. "What the hell did he mean by that?" Too late! The elevator light read "lobby." I exited only to see what Ralph meant. There stood an exceedingly long-haired, much younger man. Immediately, Matt reminded me of the old David Lee Roth video "Just a Gigolo." "In a bizarre way," I thought to myself, "compared to what I am looking at, I would have preferred Louie Prima." Somewhere in the recesses of my mind, I remember my father instructing me, after countless times of playing that song in my room as a seventeen-year-old-kid, that it was Louie Prima who originally wrote that piece in the late forties. I'd never seen a picture of Louie Prima, but I think he would have been better than Matt.

As I approached Matt, I quickly registered his apparel. From the unnecessarily long, stringy hair down to the gaudy snakeskin boots, I was utterly repulsed. Fabio, this guy was not. Upon closer inspection, his leather jacket was ancient, and fringed in all the wrong places! What set me reeling with disgust was the overly obnoxious, sophomoric chain attached to his back pocket, which was probably attached to an equally obnoxious motorcycle-logoed wallet, I imagined. What put me over the top were the cutoff leather gloves he wore as he reached out to shake my hand. I reticently shook his hand, only to detect the overwhelming stench of cheap whiskey and flounder (it could have been a fluke, but I could not discern). Now the pitchfork was firmly stuck in my neck. I could hear that little diablo laughing at me as we left the lobby. For some reason, I instinctively looked over my left shoulder, only to see Ralph laughing, as well as waving "ta-ta" in his good-natured way. If only I could crawl inside the empty soda can standing upright on the curb, I would be happier than to go through this date.

Silence was never my forte, but tonight, that's all I considered. Matt led the way conversationally. As a matter of fact, he wouldn't shut up. The old adage silence is golden really made sense to me that night. How anybody could walk that fast and talk that quickly was beyond me. He had to have snorted something, because he never exhaled for the whole twelve blocks. Cabs were nonexistent that night, and the thought of boarding a bus with this guy brought back memories of the film *One Flew over the Cuckoo's Nest*, where Jack Nicholson's character, along with the other patients and inmates, were stuck on a bus.

He said he had chosen his favorite restaurant in midtown for dinner. Great! I thought I was on my way to some greasy spoon diner with incessant Elvis playing in the background. Before we knew it, we were standing in front of Chico's—a Harley Davidson Café—wannabe in the high 40s and Tenth Avenue. Sure, there was no Elvis playing. AC/DC and Motley Crue were blaring out on the street. To believe I would have to stand in a line to get into a place like this was unimaginable (not to mention that the degrees never rose, nor did I feel warmer after a twelve-block jaunt). Out of nowhere, an enormous tattooed man in a tank top motioned for us to come forward off the line. "No waitin' fa you, my brotha. Go right in." Matt never explained his relationship with this man, nor did I want to know.

Once seated, I realized what it might be like to sit in "Biker Heaven" (my Hell!). Everywhere I looked there were motorcycle parts, guitars, and music memorabilia hanging askew. Wonderful, I thought to myself, while staring at a Steppenwolf poster where John Kay and his group gave the finger in unison to the viewer. My mind raced. How do I get myself out of this one? Do I use a toothache, a headache, a backache, or perhaps menstrual cramps (which no man can ever understand)? What made things worse was overhearing a couple seated behind us talking about the New York Taxi and Limousine Commission calling a strike earlier that evening.

"How do you like this place?" Matt interrupted.

"Interesting, if you're into all this," I responded.

"How can ya not be?" He yelled, "Waitress, two double J.D.'s straight up."

I didn't know what a J.D. was, nor did I want one at the time, let alone a double to boot. This guy had some nerve. He was ordering me what he was drinking, which was probably some awful whiskey. But with the clientele around me, I decided not to cause a stir. If J.D. was whatever he reeked of, what was the God-awful fish smell I had detected in the lobby? I decided to ask him there and then. He laughed at first and proceeded to explain. He was part owner of a fish market on South Street. He continued to describe the family-owned business, begun in the late 1800s, he being the fourth generation. At a breakneck pace, he ranted about fish, motorcycles, and his favorite movie, *Easy Rider*. I found myself nodding like a demented workhorse stranded in a pasture.

After an hour and a half of this tortuous monologue, I reminded Matt that I needed to get home since I had work the next day. "So soon?" he yelped, "the party's only beginning." That was it; it was now or never. I had to put my foot down. I told Matt no, which he apparently was unaccustomed to hearing. I even offered to pay for the meal as long as we could leave at that point. I noticed a complete change in his countenance. He was as red as a tomato.

"I may look like a derelict to you, but I make six figures, and I run a fish company at South Street Seaport. I can at least afford to pay for dinner!"

Smiling warmly, I apologized for my curtness.

"Don't worry about it," Matt said, "I've been through this before." After a couple more exchanges, Matt politely offered to walk me home. I told him it wasn't necessary because I knew the bus schedule, and if I hurried I could get the 10:35 south.

"You don't mind?" Matt asked.

"Not at all, so enjoy yourself. You look like you're in heaven here."

"Sorry it didn't work out, Trish."

Before I knew it, I was standing at the bus stop waiting for the bus to arrive. "With a little luck," I thought, "the MTA won't also be on strike." After ten minutes of shifting my weight from one foot to the other and a hundred "brrrrr's" in between, the bus pulled up and the door opened.

"Warm enough for you?" the bus driver asked. All I could do was smile, find my metro card and take the nearest available seat. The bus and the people were inviting. Before I knew it, I was a block from my apartment building. The frigid temperature slapped me as I exited the bus. I scurried as quickly as I could to my apartment building, only to find Ralph finishing a cigarette as he held the door open for me.

"Home early?" he asked.

"I'll tell you tomorrow, Ralph; I am just too tired and cold to talk about it."

As I approached the elevator, I thought I heard Ralph make a "vroom vroom" noise the way a five-year-old would, playing with his toy motorcycle. I couldn't wait to get into my pajamas and warm bed.

18

Don't Date Someone Who Lives at Work

April 2001

As seasons change, so do people. I am no exception. In my brief thirty-four years on the planet, I have learned that my persona is multifaceted. Coincidentally, my inner selves emerge with each equinox and solstice. With the impending spring of the year 2001, I found myself going through another change. I realized that my winter wasteland with the artistic types had not been productive (or at least, not at that point in my life). It was back to the nine-to-five types.

Ted responded to my profile with a very "normal" e-mail. He wrote that he worked at a well-known New York university as a sports coordinator. As a hobby, he enjoyed playing the guitar and would regularly get together with a few guys to jam. He came from a well-to-do family from Greenwich. The father, a renowned pediatrician, also taught premed courses at a local university. His mother was a registered nurse at his father's hospital. Ted claimed that his parents met when his father was an intern and his mother was a candy striper at the same hospital in which they both still work. I thought to myself, "A musician with two medically trained parents living in Greenwich—what could go wrong there?" Having experienced the admirable study of nursing for two years, I immediately felt good vibes.

We exchanged pleasant phone calls during the week. Each time we spoke, however, his cell phone would break up multiple times. When I asked Ted to call me back from his home phone, I sensed his anxiety.

"Oh, alright, umm, sorry about that. I'm due for an upgrade on my cell phone anyway."

It was at that point that I knew something was off. I couldn't put my finger on it, but it was seemingly more than just a phone issue. The following morning I received another phone call from Ted, and along with it, the same problem. This time he sounded as if he was calling from Bangladesh, not from Connecticut. My curiosity got the better of me and I said, "I thought you were going to call me back on your home phone." The deafening silence that followed concerned me.

"Are you still there, Ted?" I inquired, thinking it was another cell phone reception glitch.

"I'm here," he said curtly.

I decided to let him continue the conversation, and after a pregnant pause of a good thirty-five seconds, I asked him again.

"Are you still there, Ted?"

"Yeah, I am, already!"

"Is there something wrong, Ted? Why the tentativeness?"

"Trish, something came up, ah, so I'll call you later," Ted hurried.

"Much later, hopefully," I thought to myself, "because this is getting too weird. Either he has the oldest cell phone in creation or he picks the worst places to make his calls to me." I wasn't going to give it a second thought. With Easter rapidly approaching, I turned my attention to one of my favorite holidays of the year. Not that I need an excuse to buy a new outfit (no bonnet, please), but Easter is the best time for two reasons: The pastels of the season, along with the warming weather, spell relief from the cold, dark winter that is truly behind us. Secondly, the festive notion of rebirth and renewal is what I enjoy the most. Unlike Christmas, there's less obligation, stress, tension, and the need to placate others. In addition, being single on Easter is not disparaged by others like being alone on Christmas, New Year's Eve, and Valentine's Day. I like Groundhog Day and Arbor Day for the same reason. After a four-hour Bloomingdale shopping fix, I came home with a sense of rejuvenation. Another plus resulting from impulsive shopping stints is the opportunity to donate my old and outdated clothing to charity (who am I kidding—I'll never fit into size 8 again!).

While I was rummaging and making room for my new spring ensembles, the phone began to ring. Instead of falling victim to my old bad habit of immediately answering the phone, I was willing to give my new caller ID contraption its first workout. Realizing I hadn't preset my message machine to four rings, it didn't pick up after four rings like usual. Good, I thought to myself; this gives me more time to recognize the number. No luck. I did not recognize the number. Just then the phone stopped ringing. The nice thing about this caller ID is that it immediately stores the last number until the user erases it. Walking back to my closet, I heard my cell phone ring. The same number appeared there. Who could this 212 number be? I hoped it was not another telemarketer! However, what telemarketer would know both my home and cell number? I decided to let my voice mail cover this one. A minute later, I retrieved my voice mail.

"Trish, this is Ted. I've been trying to call you over the last hour. I tried you on your home number, but you weren't there. I'm calling from home, and my cell phone's battery is charging. The number is 212—."

"That's odd, because 212," I thought to myself, "is a city number! He told me he lived in Connecticut." Now I knew that something was more than just odd with Ted. Ultimately, I decided to call information and determine what that number was. After finding out from information that the 212 number was the student union building at the university where he worked, I became overly suspicious. I decided to call him "at home."

"Ted, this is Trish. I got your message."

"Oh, Trish, I'm glad you called. I forgot to ask you a question."

"Shoot," I said.

"I've been running this by my mom and she wants to know which nursing school you attended," he said.

Running this by his mom? Which nursing school I attended? What is wrong with this guy? It was time for me to be more assertive.

"Are you at home now, Ted?" I asked.

"Yes and no."

"What do you mean? If your mom is there and she's that interested, I would love to tell her myself!"

"Ah, well, I have two homes. The one in Greenwich is more of a weekend home, and the other is temporary."

"What does that mean?" I pried.

"Umm, well, it is really hard to find a reasonably, affordable apartment in New York City, so I decided to just crash in my office at the college for a little while."

"You're kidding!" I laughed.

"Trish, college positions don't pay well."

"But, Ted, this is the weekend, so shouldn't you be up in Greenwich now?"

"Yes, but I had to work on this summer's catalog."

At that point he had redeemed himself by telling the truth. Although I found it a bit bizarre, he did sound sincere, and I still wanted to meet him.

"Trish, are we still on for brunch tomorrow?" Ted inquired.

"Yes, I will meet you at noon."

All things considered, the brunch went exceptionally well. We decided to make another date, for a dinner, and went out a few nights later for some Mexican food. We were fond of each other and continued to date. Our time together included dinner dates, nights at the theatre, the latest films, and working out at the gym. He even took me to the gym at the university where he worked. He gave me a tour of the university and confided in me that he had actually lived in his office for over a year. Over a year! Now that was really weird. What would a son of a wealthy Greenwich doctor be doing living in an 8' by 10' office? I wanted to know details, so I asked him, "How does this work?"

"You see, I keep a sleeping bag under my desk with a few changes of clothes. Since my office is next door to the gym in the sports complex, I shower in the locker room before the coaches get in at six or after everyone leaves late at night."

"What about the maintenance staff?" I queried.

"Oh, they're all friends of mine. They think I am a workaholic. I also keep my office locked."

At that point I questioned whether he was insane or just a cheapo. I concluded that he was a little of both!

Just then Ted's cell phone rang. Answering, Ted turned to me and said, "Trish, I have to take this call. It's important. It's the athletic director. I'll be back in a few minutes."

Ted scurried down the hallway and up the stairs until he disappeared. To pass the time, I checked my e-mail on his computer. As I was checking my e-mail, I noticed that his computer was part of a LAN (local area network). Out of curiosity, I checked his history. To my surprise, I found that he had visited several porn sites. Oh no, here we go again! The porn sites were mostly of barely legal teens and nurses. To think that he worked around young college students, not to mention his mother being a nurse. What would she think if she knew? When Ted came back in the room, he caught me with a horrified look on my face.

"The fact that you live in your office is one thing, but this compulsive obsession is way more than I can tolerate. I thought we discussed my legacy and bad experiences with guys much like yourself!" I bellowed.

"Wait a minute. Why are you judging me? Every guy visits porn sites once in a while," Ted retorted.

"Yes, Ted, but not sites with photos of barely legal teens and nurses. Your mother certainly wouldn't approve, would she?"

"Well, that was a low blow," Ted snorted.

"Talk about an Oedipus complex," I thought to myself. The situation was really getting freaky.

"Look, I am not looking for sympathy; I got kicked out of my home for this and other things," Ted replied.

"I don't care to know the details. Your computer is part of a LAN. People lose their jobs every day due to company-installed spyware programmed to catch people like you," I informed him.

"You're making me out to be a criminal. What do you mean by 'people like you'?"

"Sorry, Ted, it is getting out of control. I am supersensitive about this sort of thing. I know that, although you made a few bad choices, you're right. You're not a criminal. I have no right to judge you."

"Maybe you should just go," Ted concluded.

As I walked to the subway, I began to resign myself to the thought that the world was filled with misfit boys like the misfit toys in the classic tale *Pinocchio*. Then again, at least it was obvious when Pinocchio told a lie.

19

Don't Date a Biter

April 2003

Nearing the one-year anniversary of 9/11, the most heinous attack ever made on American soil, I slowly emerged from the cocoon I had unconsciously spun. Most New Yorkers, at first, rallied around each other and became closer in the months following the attack. However, as the year progressed, I noticed more and more of my fellow New Yorkers detaching themselves from each other in the effort to insulate against the horrors they had suffered. I too became more and more distant as the months elapsed. After watching one of the most important financial buildings belonging not only to New York City but also to the world, destroyed in a matter of minutes, my sense of self-importance and need for companionship paled by comparison. Internet dating was the last thing that concerned me at that point in my life. However, after a year and a half of quiet solace, I decided that loneliness and self-denial would never bring back the thousands of lives lost or the buildings that were destroyed. Solitude solves nothing, I decided.

It was at that time I decided to reenter the electronic dating game. I received a very romantic response to my profile from an Italian man named Paulo from Rome. He wrote that he had enjoyed my profile the most because it was filled with richness of culture, passion, and adventure. He explained that the majority of American women seemed very cynical and lacked creativity. The image Paulo attached was as qualitative as any I have ever seen on the cover of GQ. Dark hair, piercing green eyes, five-o'clock shadow, just the right amount of chest hair, and toned biceps protruding from his designer white T-shirt completed the picture. Studying architecture at Cooper Union on a scholarship,

Paulo appeared much younger than his stated age of thirty years. Although most people would have given their right arm to excel in the family-owned olive oil business as Paulo claimed he did, he had decided that a second career was in order. As a child, he had proven his love for Venetian architecture to anyone who knew him. Paulo described his summers in Sicily and his winters in Palermo from the ages of six through twelve. From the articulated sand castles to the dioramas he constructed, Paulo's love of architecture was noteworthy. It was time, at the age of thirty, to pursue his first love. He stated that there were very few students near his age. As a result, he considered online dating. After a few good experiences, he was looking for a great experience.

We spoke on the phone and our conversation lasted for over an hour. His Italian accent allowed me the opportunity to fantasize enjoying espresso at a corner café like the ones in the Piazza Navona. Perhaps riding a Vespa on the Isle of Capri or even sailing through the canals of Venice in a gondola might cure what had previously ailed me. Even just the beautiful change of scenery could lift my spirits and drag me out of the destructive doldrums that had plagued me over the past six months. Nevertheless, we agreed to meet at a beautiful, architecturally sound Catholic Church close by. Paulo had chosen this church because of its traditional Italian motif.

As I approached the church, I saw Paulo sitting on the third step, smoking a cigarette, Leonardo DiCaprio—like. He wore the same ensemble that he had worn in the photo he sent me. However, he forgot to mention that he was only 5'7". Had I known, being five foot ten inches, I would have worn flats that day. Instead, in the heels I had chosen, I now loomed nearly six inches over him. Nonetheless, I enjoyed our conversation immensely. He asked me if I would be interested in seeing the inside of St. Francis of Padua's chapel, to which I responded, "Certainly. Not only have I heard mass here before, but I've attended a christening here as well."

"In that case would you be willing to give me a private tour?" Paulo asked warmly.

"By all means," I responded.

After forty-five minutes of a bulging-eyed Paulo and countless "oohs" and "ahs," we exited the church, this time through the rear door behind the altar.

"I don't know what is more beautiful, you or the church," Paulo exclaimed.

At that point his height was no longer an issue, for his words and sentiments were big enough to compensate. Enjoying ourselves greatly, we agreed to meet for dinner two nights later.

We planned to meet at a restaurant of his choice, a trendy hot spot. This time, I wore stylish flats and a pretty sundress. We sat down, and he ordered some wine without even asking if I wanted any, and started to flatter me, Italian-style. We shared appetizers, and he fed me breadsticks. Right before the main course arrived, he told me that I had very cute cheeks.

"Your cheeks are so cute, I would like to bite them," Paulo proclaimed.

"Are you serious? I don't think that's a good idea, Paulo," I retorted.

In the midst of questioning his motives, Paulo seized the opportunity, and actually bit my right cheek quite firmly! Shocked and a tad disorientated, I excused myself and made haste to the restroom.

As I stood in front of the mirror, I watched my cheek turn a deep purple as teeth marks from both his upper and lower jaw appeared. At this point, the pain became quite intense and sharp. I rummaged through my purse to find the strongest painkiller I had with me. There it was: Extra Strength Excedrin. After washing it down with some water, I headed back to the table to inform Paulo that I didn't appreciate his love bite. I demanded both an explanation and an apology. He neither apologized nor explained his behavior. Normally a pacifist, I was so incensed that I wanted to haul off and hit him with my handbag. He thought it was no big deal and actually laughed about it. I told him this was outrageous, and I didn't know what they did in Italy, but in America it is unacceptable to bite your date.

Riding home in a cab I wondered what I would tell my colleagues and students tomorrow. I also pondered if I still had any leftover penicillin from last winter when I had had a sinus infection. If I did, the first order of business would be to swallow two pills and then ice my face to bring down the swelling. How dare he! Who the hell did he think he was? Considering that his height was only five foot seven inches, I wondered if I should have told him about my three brothers who range in height from six foot two inches to six foot four inches, with weights of over 250 pounds!! Who knows, maybe Paulo might have bitten one of them on the kneecap, to make matters worse than they already were.

20

It's a Small World After All

November 2003

Realizing that I had bitten off more than I could chew, I turned my attention to the beginnings of another school year. As I mentioned earlier, the beginning of most school years has more work than any other time in the term. As most teachers will tell you, they need a good two months to get comfortable with the new class, parents, and recently hired staff members comprising the school environment. Normally, this comfort zone arrived much sooner than the Thanksgiving break. However, this year was different because I was teaching the first grade! And this was no ordinary first-grade class; I was to teach children with developmental delays. Since my degree qualified me to teach in this area, the district invited me to take the challenge. Not only would I have to learn a new curriculum, but I also would have to relocate to another classroom in another wing of the building. To make matters more complicated, some of these students had not attended kindergarten the year before. This was the best time to focus on my career and a better time to leave Internet dating alone.

Slowly but surely the winds of November blew the leaves off the trees. "My God," I said to myself, "where did the last three months go?" Before long, Thanksgiving, Christmas, and New Year's would arrive. Great! It would be another holiday season without the festivities. I couldn't remember when I had last enjoyed a truly Merry Christmas or a really Happy New Year's Eve, and now I was facing another lonely holiday season. During my first six years of living in Chelsea, there had always been lonely-looking little old women living next to me. These old gals had survived their husbands by at least a dozen years, but I often wondered how they survived the holidays. Occasionally I would witness the token appearance of one of these ladies' daughters or granddaughters or some other relative, giving me the standard, "Happy Holidays." Come to think of it, I had noticed many other mature ladies frequenting the elevator and lobby of my building, to the point that I asked Ralph, the doorman (a New York historian in his own right) about this phenomenon. As he laughed, he told me that I needed to research the few blocks I walked each day.

"Why should I, Ralph?" I inquired.

"Don't you know this is Spinster Heaven, Trish?" Ralph answered. "I hope you won't be a member of the chosen few club," Ralph added as he opened the door and smiled at an old woman with packages in tow.

I watched this transaction in sheer horror! I saw myself coming through a similar door (if not the same door) in the distant future, with an ancient Ralph assisting me with my little Yorkshire Terrier and shopping bags full of unnecessary gaudy clothing. "That's it," I said to myself. "I am going back upstairs to my Internet dating habit. Spinsterhood is not for me!"

After posting my profile once again, I researched the community now called Chelsea. I learned that back in the forties and fifties, before Chelsea's alternative/bohemian lifestyle of the seventies, eighties, and nineties, this was an enclave of professionals "on their way to the top." In the forties and fifties, dentists, doctors and CPAs in the midst of their careers gravitated to Chelsea. Most of the buildings in the area were zoned professional and residential, including my apartment building. My apartment in particular had been a dentist's office in the late fifties. I only learned this after tearing up the grotesque lime green rug and noticing on the hardwood floors the markings of what were once partitioned walls separating the examining room from the waiting room. After asking my landlady, who had owned my co-op, she confirmed my suspicion by telling me that her father was the dentist who practiced there. She also added that her mother worked as his receptionist and nurse. She spoke fondly of the apartment and reminisced about the many times she had sat on the floor of what became my galley kitchen. She rambled on incessantly about the innocent days where she would wait patiently for her parents to finish their workday, playing with her dolls and coloring for hours. What struck me while she spoke was the fact that people back then needed much less to get by. I came to the conclusion that I would never complain again to anyone about how small my apartment was.

Ironically, the next day, as I boarded the elevator from the lobby, I encountered an odd-looking man smiling awkwardly. Introducing himself as Michael, and enlarging an awkward smile, he spoke of his newness to the building and expressed a yearning to meet people. He was either high on life or laughing gas, and his smile made me uncomfortable. I immediately categorized him as an out-of-towner, maybe from somewhere out west or even Canada. In New York people don't smile at all, especially at strangers for no apparent reason. I politely said hello to him and attempted to end the greeting there. When he pressed the sixteenth floor button, I just knew that he was my new neighbor. I got off the elevator and proceeded to unlock my apartment door. To my surprise, he was standing next to me, still with an increasingly disturbing grin as he said, "I'm right next door, isn't that funny?" Funny was the last thing I was thinking. It was scary maybe, but certainly not funny.

Thinking about the way I looked, as most women do on a regular basis, I realized that my appearance was less than desirable. "Great," I thought to myself, "this would have to be the day that I rushed home from the gym without my usual locker room shower, deciding to wait for the comfort of my own tub." With my hair tied in a severe ponytail under a foolish-looking baseball cap, I realized my appearance must have been ghastly. I wasn't in the mood for any new encounters. Nonetheless, he seemed harmless. I guessed the little old lady next to me had either passed away or moved down to Miami, where they have bingo every Wednesday. It's amazing that in New York City, one could live next door to another person and not even know his or her name, nor care to know it.

After a relaxing bath, I resigned myself to checking my online dating site. By the time I had logged on, I realized the irony of my screen name, which read "Girl Next Door in NYC." A few days later, while checking my responses, I surprisingly discovered an e-mail from my new neighbor, Mike. He didn't write anything about recognizing me or knowing me; he simply sent a "form" e-mail that he may have sent to any number of women. Laughing out loud, I felt the need to respond. Returning the e-mail, I mentioned, "As my screen name says, I actually *am* the 'Girl Next Door'!" "To refresh your memory, we met on the elevator just a few days ago."

At that moment, I could picture Mike reading the e-mail and saying, "Well, golly gee," as his smile got even wider. He wrote back, asking if I cared to meet him for a drink. I thought about how easy and convenient it would be. But with added thought, I decided that I didn't feel a connection, and it wasn't just his excessive smiling. I wrote back: "Thanks, but maybe we can meet sometime down the road instead."

Like a bad cold sore, I couldn't shake Mike for anything. No matter how kind I was, he insisted we meet for something. What puzzled me, however, was that his requests were always electronic. I never heard him knock on my door. I am not complaining, mind you. But this is the nature of cyberdating. Mike knew the rules. I developed a newfound respect for him in the way he allowed me my space. He could have been a nuisance, since we were living so close, but I must say one thing for him: he was a gentleman and knew his place.

Mercifully, I didn't see him in the building for approximately two weeks. Once again, on the way to the gym on a Saturday morning (just like the first time I had met him), he entered the elevator, but this time he was with a woman who could have passed for his sister.

He greeted me with a great big, "Hello, Trish. This is Samantha."

"Hi, Samantha, nice to meet you," I said.

Mike proceeded to tell me that Samantha hailed from two towns north of Omaha—his own hometown. She had just moved to New York.

"That's nice. Where did the two of you meet?" I inquired.

"We met while line dancing at the Gold Rush last weekend," Mike proudly responded.

What made me smile (but not as wide as they were smiling) was their outright similarity. Their smiles were identical! No wonder they grew up in the same area. What a wonderful thing it must be to smile for no apparent reason. Or maybe they had a reason. Maybe that old saying holds more weight than I thought: there's a key for every lock. This instilled the strangest sense of hope in me. I had never felt so elated during my years of cyberdating than I did that morning.

PART II
Hope Prevails

21

Finally! My Internet Date from Heaven

November 2003

After what appeared to be a lifetime of miscues in the game of dating, I had nearly resigned myself to the thought that I was destined to be single. "Single, hmmm," I thought to myself. That didn't sound so bad. I could come and go as I pleased and not have to answer to anyone. If I wanted to eat ice cream for breakfast every day for a year, I could do so without an onlooker criticizing my mental health. I could miss my weekly housecleaning chores without reprisal from an overzealous, anal-retentive husband. I could date whomever I wished, without worrying about food expenses (missing out on, particularly, that wonderful experience of standing in line with all the other miserable housewives at the local supermarket). Single! It sounded better and better the more I said it. I wouldn't have to deal with annoying in-laws and wouldn't have to attend infinitely boring family outings.

But then again, it would be tough during the holidays. Those damn holidays! I couldn't seem to evade them. Just to think it had been only six short years ago that I had found myself reveling in holidays like Christmas with its mistletoe and yuletide cheer, New Year's, with its noisemakers and silly hats, and Valentine's Day with its pink hearts and candy assortments. After a year of near hits (if not near misses), I considered reentering the harried world of Internet dating one last time. I knew I had said "one last time" before, so this time, I would use the word "final." Final!! There, I said it. My only problem with this word was its finality. I was never a final-type girl. I had always had hope for myself and for my fellow man. But before I would waste another six long years, I needed to draw the line in the sand.

An odd sense of hope enveloped me while changing my old screen name to a more subtle screen name. My new screen name really spelled it all out. How could any red-blooded American male refuse? I changed my "Girl Next Door in NYC" screen name to "Nordic Angel."

Thinking of all the lessons I had learned regarding mistakes or miscalculations, I pondered using my newfound knowledge to keep from getting sucked into another hellish date or relationship. My next step was to make a list of how I would do things differently. Reviewing everything that had transpired over the last six years, I prioritized based on importance, to create my own little top five list. This doesn't mean that I disregarded everything else I had learned. Instinctively I made sure that my potential date had a variety of recent photos attached, and I made sure that there was at least one head shot without a hat or sunglasses obscuring his true identity.

Number one on my list was to not accept e-mails that were outside the tri-state area. As much as men from foreign lands intrigued me, both my budget and patience were worn out regarding the travel issue. Number two was that the guy needed to have been in previous long-term relationships. Number three was to select men who were neither flashy nor pretentious. Next was to select a family-oriented man with a future in mind. Finally (I know I already used that word), I would select someone who shared his love for the arts with others. The other lessons that I had learned based on my experiences would have to be tested via the telephone and the first date.

Returning home from visiting friends in Philadelphia with my best friend Greg, I rushed into my apartment to a ringing telephone. Much to my chagrin, it was just another telemarketer hawking some useless product. Taking off my coat, I instinctively turned on my computer. As I signed on to my Internet provider, I heard the ever-familiar sound, "You've got mail." Boy did I! I had fifty-two responses alone that day, and one-hundred-forty-one over the past three days! "Wow, I guess that new screen name worked," I thought to myself.

Recognizing the large number of responses, I slowly scrolled through them. One in particular caught my eye. It was from a gentleman named Tom from New Jersey. "Hmm, New Jersey," I thought to myself. "That settles my first concern." After this, I looked at Tom's age. This guy was two years my senior. I read on, discovering that he was previously involved in a few long-term relationships, so the prior relationships concern was also satisfied. After divulging his nonmarital status, I felt most comfortable. While reading farther, I determined that Tom's response was creatively personal, like no other that I had ever received before.

> Subj: **WOW—What a Profile**
> Date: 11/02/2003 10:00:40 PM Eastern Daylight Time
> From: uofatom88
> To: NordicAngel
>
> Hi,
>
> Your username and photo caught my eye. You mention in your profile that your legs are your best feature, but I couldn't get a clear view in the photos, so I wanted to tell you that you have a beautiful face with incredible blue eyes.
>
> I read your profile.... WOW, you sound like an absolutely amazing woman with an incredible appetite for travel and culture. There isn't anything on the list that I wouldn't enjoy doing myself. Being born in Germany and moving 10 times during the first 11 years of my life, traveling was ingrained in my brain. I lived in Germany in the early 90's and began traveling extensively through Europe. Now I make a trip every summer exploring a new corner of the continent. I've been to some of the places on your list including Zermatt, Venice, Pisa (one of your photos), and Tuscany.
>
> In fact this past summer, I rented a convertible and toured the wine country of Umbria and Tuscany for a week and then went to the Island of Sardinia for a week long biking trip with some close friends and family.
>
> I am extremely family oriented and have a great relationship with my immediate family and all of my relatives. I see my father, who lives 10 minutes away, at least once a week. Even though my sister and her husband live in Boulder, CO, I still get out there twice a year. In fact I'll be there over Thanksgiving.
>
> What type of photography do you do? I always wanted to get into some serious photography after taking a class in college, but never took the time. Now I just use my digital camera with reckless abandon. I think I have a pretty good eye for composition, due to my architectural background. I earned a Bachelors in Architecture from the University of Arizona.
>
> What's the significance of your username? Are you or your relatives from Scandinavia? I would love to hear back from you.
>
> Tom

Referring to several exotic locales that I had listed in my ad, I sensed a connection. That took care of my fifth request. He obviously enjoyed culture. Expressing his fondness for his family, I sensed his paternal instinct loud and clear. Tom even stated that he was a man not afraid to get married. That about wrapped it up! Now for the icing on the cake, I thought to myself as I downloaded his photo attachments. I realized after viewing half of the available shots, that half was enough. Although on the thin side, he was not only trim, but also fit. His attractiveness enthralled me. He was dressed comfortably and casually. What got me was that he was smiling in all the photos, and not posing awkwardly or rigidly like most men did in their online photos. That did it! That satisfied number three. No more flashy or pretentious men! The more time I spent looking at his photos and rereading his email, I came to the realization that he was different, in a good way.

I noticed that Tom had sent the e-mail days before. Since I was away for the weekend and did not have Internet access, I hadn't responded earlier. I made haste in answering his e-mail. I wasted no time in giving him both my home and cell phone numbers. Even though giving out my phone number was always a no-no, I made an exception this time. All I could think of was reeling in this keeper.

With a combination of fatigue and newfound hope, I focused on getting a good night's rest and anticipating the work week along with his call. In an effort to defray any unnecessary late chitchat with my friend Charlene, I shut my cell phone off and put my home phone on answering machine mode (after one ring).

As fate would have it, I slept like a log. Eight hours went by like eight minutes. I can't remember the last time I slept that soundly! Normally I am up at least one or two times for a variety of reasons. Since the sun hadn't come up yet (because November in New York is the second darkest month of the year due to daylight savings time), I triple-checked my clock radio to make sure it was 5:30 AM. Then I hit the floor running. Before I knew it, I was in my car heading toward the Midtown tunnel, humming an old Police song, "Message in a Bottle." Over and over again I sang the words, "Sending out an SOS." By the third time, my cell phone rang. Since I was already halfway through the tunnel, the cell screen displayed "No Service." "Damn," I thought to myself. "Who the hell could that be at this early hour in the morning?" There's only one thing worse than a late night phone call, and it's the evil twin—the early morning one. They both spell trouble. By the time I emerged on the Long Island City side of the tunnel, I calmed myself and became more focused with the day ahead. No one in *his* right mind would call me at this time of the day, or would he?

I nervously attached my hands-free phone earplugs in the event that the caller would try again. Before Sting could get the second chorus of "Roxanne" out, the phone rang. "It's him," I thought despairingly. But it wasn't. It was just my friend Charlene, also a fellow teacher, calling to inform me that she had just called in sick and was wondering if I could help the sub find her emergency plans.

"No problem," I answered. "Do you have bus duty today? In that case, I'll call you at 3:30. Feel better," I added.

"Phew," I thought to myself. "Thank God, it wasn't Tom. I don't know what I would have done if it were."

The day went by without a hitch. Charlene's succinct plans were in the top drawer of her desk, where she feared they weren't. The sub needed no assistance. Just as well, I thought to myself. Looking at Charlene's replacement, I thought, where on earth did they dig up this old fossil? She had to be at least eighty-two years old! Just like the night's sleep, the day went smoothly. I was in the car headed home when I turned on my cell phone. I noticed that I had two messages! Impulsively listening, at first I couldn't identify the voice, but then he said his name was Tom. He asked me to call him back on his cell or his work number. I decided to wait until I got home to make the call. To this day I even remember the time I called him—4:45 PM—just catching him before he left work.

The conversation went well and we spoke for over an hour. I know that I recommended keeping the first phone conversation short; however, in this case I made an exception because our conversation felt so natural. I used the opportunity to learn more about Tom. For instance, he lived on his own and was a homeowner. That cleared my concern regarding men still living at home with their parents. I also found out that Tom was born and raised in Hamburg, Germany. His voice was pleasing. I sensed a slight accent. He was certainly scoring points in my book! As we chatted, as crazy as this sounds, I couldn't think of anything other than the possibility of him being my future husband. I know I have said this before, but this time I actually felt it. As we spoke, I looked at his picture, and I could sense an immediate bond. We felt equally comfortable discussing everything from music to family to films, and we planned to meet that coming Tuesday.

Due to some poorly prepared Indian cuisine that I had insisted on having the night before, I awoke to terrible stomach pains. "Great," I thought to myself, "I'm going to have to cancel what might be the most important date in the last six years." I called Tom from work to ask for a rain check. I sensed some disappointment in his voice. To provide some reassurance that I was still interested in meeting, I told him that we could talk on the phone after he left work. With a little help from some antacids, I endured a full day at school. What a difference a day makes. The day before couldn't have run more smoothly, but the following day was miserable. There was nothing worse than little children buzzing around my desk when I had the ever-present fear of diarrhea, and to make matters worse, that year I wasn't assigned a teacher's assistant to relieve me. Deciding that the trip back to the city would be too precarious, I called my folks and beseeched them to let me stay the night. I promised I would stay far away from them, as long as a toilet was nearby. They agreed, as long as I stayed in the upstairs bedroom.

As luck would have it, Tom showed his true colors by calling three times, each time to see if I was feeling better than the last time. Again, our conversation just flowed naturally. After the battery in my cell phone died, I switched to my parents' home phone. I didn't realize how late it was until my mother picked up the phone to make a call and rudely interrupted me with "Trish, are you still on the phone? Remember, you need to get some sleep to let your body recover." I was quite embarrassed and apologized to Tom. He told me not to worry and that it was sweet that my mom was so concerned. Before we said our good-byes, we agreed to meet for brunch on the coming Saturday.

Saturday came and he called to inform me that he was in front of my apartment building. I broke out in a cold sweat from nerves as I made my way down in the elevator. I exited my building and caught a glimpse of him standing next to his car with flowers in hand. He was even more handsome than any of the photos that I had seen.

While greeting each other, he handed me the flowers. As he opened the door, I sensed my nervousness increase. I thought to myself, "This man obviously has good manners," while I thanked him and told him that I had to run back up to my apartment to put the flowers in water. I thought, "This could buy me some calm down time."

As I returned to the elevator doing an involuntary odd dance, Ralph smiled at me and said, "Trish, does this one have potential?"

"Like no one else, Ralph," I exclaimed as I pressed the elevator button to my floor.

"Flowers on the first date! Boy, that guy has some class!" Ralph proclaimed.

As the elevator doors were closing behind me, I loudly blurted, "I think we have found the one Ralph!" Once in my apartment, I composed myself, only to realize that I might be going on my very last first date. This is the kind of moment that changes one's life forever I thought. Immediately I felt the onset of an anxiety attack. It didn't make sense to me, for this is what I was looking for. Having it made me panic-stricken. Apparently, I had spent the last six years in an unreal world. This adult dose of reality drove me to fear.

"Are you nervous?" I asked as I entered Tom's car.

"Of course, aren't you?" he said.

"Yes, so am I," I answered.

What was I afraid of? What was he nervous about? What was wrong with us? We both laughed and immediately were at ease. Miraculously, by New York City standards, we managed to find a parking spot right in front of the restaurant. After several lines of meaningless banter and a giggle here or there, we simultaneously caught each other staring. It was at that point we realized we had to step up to the plate. No more batting practice. The game was on!

After we were seated, our conversation flowed so well that we sent the waiter away three times because we were nowhere near ready to order. I guess that semi-serious stare/laughter did the trick. This situation called for concentration. Although we were hungry, food was not the main objective that afternoon. It took us thirty minutes before we ever even opened the menu, and, due to our mutual attraction, to this day neither one of us can remember what we ate.

"I can't remember the last time I was this comfortable with someone on a first date, can you?" Tom asked.

Thinking carefully before I answered and probably taking too much time, Tom grabbed my hand and asked me what was taking so long. It was just the touch of his hand that guaranteed me the sincerity and kindness that I had never experienced before. I finally felt at home, exactly where I was supposed to be. Ironically a tear appeared on my left cheek. I say ironic because it was he that discovered it, not I.

"What's wrong? Am I going too fast? Take as much time as you need," he concluded.

I was lip-locked. I couldn't speak if I had to. A knot appeared in my esophagus and the waterworks began to flow. I looked through my veil of tears just to see a horrified Tom. It looked like he was going to have a stroke.

"Please, Trisha, say something, anything. Tell me to go away or even shut up!"

It was at this moment I began to lose my self-security. I don't remember if I excused myself or not, but I bolted to the ladies' room in record time. Luckily, it was empty. Like a teenager, I locked myself in one of the stalls and had the following argument with myself. I think I said the following:

"What the hell is the matter with you, Trish? Why are you acting like this? This feeling is exactly what you've wanted to feel all your life. You'll be damn lucky if he's still sitting where you left him if you have enough guts to get off this toilet."

It was at that time I heard the door open and saw the appearance of two black sneakers.

"Excuse me, Miss, your date wants to know if you're OK." an apparent waitress inquired.

"Thank you so much," I said while I opened the stall door, "I just got cold feet and I don't know why," I blurted.

"It's OK, happens to best of us."

As she led me out of the bathroom, she reminded me that my mascara was a mess. Boy was she right. Although I was looking at myself in the mirror, Elvira the vampire-like Queen of Halloween, was looking back at me.

"You have some?" she asked as she pointed to her own eye makeup. It was at that point I felt most comfortable, but looked horrible. I demurely nodded to her. She said good luck and asked if there was anything she could do for me. I was so choked with emotion, I could hardly speak; therefore, I merely waved good-bye. Her warm smile and gentle nod assured me I was in a good place in more ways than one. I rapidly repaired with Revlon and exited the restroom.

As fate would have it, Dean Martin's "Amore" was playing. I began to laugh out loud, causing a couple of waiters and at least one cook to stare. I couldn't help but recall my two older brothers would sing their version of this song, which was vulgar, yet hysterical. I couldn't stop laughing all the way to the table.

The look on Tom's face was one of sheer confusion.

"Are you feeling all right? We can leave," he said.

"No, I just needed a moment. I was overwhelmed with the level of comfort that you offered. I know it sounds like a cliché, but I feel like we were meant to meet. To be honest, I panicked."

It was his turn to grow silent. Suddenly I returned the favor and without hesitation I reached over and grabbed his hand. Seconds later Tom leaned over and kissed my cheek as he whispered in my ear, "Thank God, you feel the same way as I do."

It was Tom's turn to open the flood gates. He talked incessantly for a least forty minutes—everything from modern architecture, to Munich, Germany, to the New York Mets, to pistachio ice cream and then some. We even compared our misguided dating stories. He confided in me about his last relationship and how it felt empty and that he was looking not for someone he could live with, but for someone he couldn't live without.

Although I normally would have suggested ending the date after a brief encounter, I followed my gut and agreed to prolong our meeting because we had already spent countless hours on the phone, and he seemed to be passing every test. All of my fears and concerns were disappearing. Exchanging travel stories, we walked a few blocks and enjoyed the rest of the afternoon strolling through Central Park. He asked if I had ever taken one of the buggy rides at Christmastime. I sensed some permanence here since it was only November and I had to get through Thanksgiving first. I lied and said no and asked had he.

"No, I always wanted to go with someone special, but never felt a strong enough connection with anyone," Tom stated.

"Yes, I agree. These romantic events need to be shared with the right person," I remarked.

"Do you have plans for December?" Tom whispered.

"Yes," I unconsciously created a pregnant pause. After a few seconds I said, "With you, of course."

The sweet smile on his face warmed me as we leisurely finished our walk through Central Park. But as all good things do, this date too had to end. Both of us had already made other commitments for that evening. Tom had to attend a black tie affair with his two bosses and their wives, and I had planned to have dinner with Greg. Tom drove me back to my apartment and walked me to the door. It must have been the first time in a very long time that I felt extreme sadness as we said our good-byes. A nice hug, a kiss on the cheek, and a wave as he got back into his car. My body was overcome with a variety of emotions ranging from extreme happiness to sadness, but mainly happiness. As I passed Ralph, on the way to the elevator, he proclaimed, "Must have been a pretty good date considering how long you were out."

"You don't know how good!" I exclaimed.

I decided to let Ralph in on the details at another time. I was too excited about the time I had just spent with Tom and wanted to tell Greg all about it now, rather than waiting until dinner. I spent the next three hours in Greg's apartment recapping everything that took place that afternoon. Greg could barely get a word in the entire time, but he didn't mind, since he hadn't seen me that happy in quite some time.

Ever the gentleman, Tom called the very next day to thank me for a wonderful first date. I kept thinking it was I that had reason to be thankful. Little did he know, at that time, how many dates from hell I had been through in the previous six years. After recounting some of the previous day's highlights, he went on to tell me that he had decided to hide his profile, since he didn't want to date anyone else. I was blown away. How could he be so serious so quickly?

I asked him, "Are you sure?"

"I have never been more sure of anything in my life," he responded. "I feel extremely comfortable when I'm with you; it is as if we have known each other for much longer."

"It is as if our souls have been apart and now helped us find each other," I added.

"I guess that is what they mean by soul mates," he finished my thought.

Here I was, more than six years of Internet dating, and I had finally found what I was always looking for. I couldn't believe how lucky Tom was, since I had been his first and only Internet date.

Falling in love over the course of four months, Tom proposed to me at One if by Land, Two if by Sea, a historic carriage house converted to the most romantic restaurant in New York City. The proposal was followed by a horse and buggy ride in Central Park. Only five months later, we were married in St. Patrick's Cathedral and remain happy to this day.

Fairy tales really do come true. The most important lesson that I have learned is not to give up hope. Never give up hope that you will find your partner, bringing your search to an end. Like Emily Dickinson said, "Hope is the thing with feathers that perches in the soul."

Finally! My Internet Date from Heaven

Part III
Posting a Personal Ad

Dos and Don'ts

Every person describes himself or herself as honest, attractive, and kind. Be more descriptive, show a photo, and let the reader be the judge of your attractiveness. If you are more than twenty pounds overweight, then state that. Some people are interested in a plus-size partner. Don't apologize for how you look. "This is who I am," should be your motto. Celebrate yourself as being unique. There is a mate for everyone. Not everyone likes the same things. The media try to dictate what is beautiful. Don't buy into it. Some men love voluptuous women, some love Asian women, and some love redheads. Some women love tall men, and some women prefer nerdy types; *no one* should dictate to you what is beautiful. You should not be a slave to fashion. You should wear what looks good on you and what celebrates your uniqueness. Strength is sexy, and self-confidence is sexy. If someone doesn't like you for some physical attribute that you have or do not have, then this person is not for you! Why should you compromise "you" for someone else? Believe that all your natural changes show the depth of your wisdom and the profoundness of your knowledge.

If You Are a Woman Seeking a Man

First, it is a must to post a recent head shot. Have the photo taken with a simple background, minus any distractions such as people or signs. Wear a simple top; black or white is best. Don't do your hair big, don't put on too much makeup, and don't wear anything too sexy unless you want only men who are looking for sex to answer your ad. Smile in your photo and show that you are approachable. If you are slim, include your weight. List what you do for a living. Include interests and pastimes. Most importantly, state what you are looking for in a mate. Post the ad and see who responds. I wouldn't recommend answering any ads if you are looking for a conventional committed relationship. Instead, let the man approach you first and then respond. Look at other women's ads and see how they are written, and then write yours differently. Your ad should be light and breezy, not heavy. The ad should not contain the following words: marriage, ex-boyfriend, ex-husband, or sex. These words are too heavy, and men don't really want to read ads that are emotionally heavy. Below are two sample ads: a do and a don't.

Do—be descriptive, show that you are fun and interesting, be unique like no other. This one is looking for a sophisticated gentleman with class and style.

5'8", fit, athletic, brunette, green-eyed, attorney, 34 years old. I have been described as cute, have a great smile and enjoy laughing. I am passionate about skiing in Vermont, sailing, dancing barefoot, world travel, wreck-diving 100 feet below, and exploring NYC. I am seeking a committed relationship with an educated self-sufficient Christian or Catholic 30–40-year-old professional. Photo a must.

Don't—be negative, sound like a gold digger or like you are full of yourself. This ad will only get low class or sexually deviant responses.

5'8", **hot** brunette, green-eyed attorney, 34 years old. I am **gorgeous** and have a **great body**. I like to ski, boat, dance, and take vacations. I am looking for a handsome **rich guy** to **spoil me rotten**. No Games Please. **Losers need not reply.**

After you receive a response from someone you wish to contact, you should not rush to respond immediately. Wait between eight and twelve hours to write back. Don't respond on a Friday or Saturday night because it will give the impression that you are lonely or desperate. You want a person to think that you are social and busy and that Internet dating is just a small part of your life. It is much more desirable for someone to think that you are popular and out and about and living your life, rather than being home in your pajamas on a Saturday night, waiting with baited breath for a response from your ad. Also, when you respond back, limit your e-mail message to a few lines, such as "Thanks for responding. I too think we may have a lot in common. What's the next step?" The object at that point is to get to know the person via phone and face-to-face, *not* to begin a pen pal relationship.

Use your ad and e-mail only as a tool toward a more reality-based introduction. Hopefully, he will write back asking for your phone number. Then you can give him your cell number and have him call you and ask you out on a real date. Men do like to pursue and, by calling you, they feel as if they are in charge. If you wish to call him instead, you can request his number and then block the number that you are calling from by pressing *67. When you speak with him, keep it under thirty minutes. You should be able to detect any negativity in that amount of time. If he puts down others or his ex or if he complains about anything, tell him that you have to go and will talk soon. You will not want to meet him if he's still upset or mad over his ex or is a negative or complaining person. If the conversation goes well and the guy asks you out, suggest that you meet for coffee or tea. Coffee is quick and you can get out of the date in less than one hour. Also, make sure that you choose a meeting place that is close to where you live. A thoughtful man will make the first move and come to you. If not, he's used to getting his way and you will not want to meet him anyway. Also, cab fare and gas can get very expensive for one coffee. If he asks you out, he should pay. Make sure that your first date is during the daytime or twilight and in a crowded place. Let a friend know whom you are meeting and give your friend your date's phone number. Let her know that you will call her when you return from the date, as a safety precaution. End the date after one hour, even if it is going well. Even before the date, you can mention that you have plans or something to do later that same day. He can always make a future date with you. If you sense that it is not going well or you don't like him, don't worry—there are plenty of fish in the sea.

If it does work out and your date seems interesting, then by all means, go out with him again. Wait at least three days. Back-to-back dates become boring and he may lose interest if you are too available. Don't e-mail or call him unless you are returning his e-mail or calls. You don't want to seem too desperate. As much as the guy likes the girl, it becomes annoying if she calls too much. He may lose interest quickly. Too many relationships end because one person smothers the other and leaves nothing to the imagination. You should still live your life, go to the gym, and meet friends for dinner in between dating. There is nothing worse than a guy thinking a woman has no one else but him.

If You Are a Man Seeking a Woman

First, you should have a recent photo. Make sure that it is a solo shot of you. Two photos are better than one. You should post one head shot and one body shot. Make sure you are wearing something casual. Jeans and a shirt are fine. Don't use a main photo where you're in a suit or a tux because it will look like you are trying too hard or it will attract gold diggers. Don't use a photo that includes your friends or one taken at a bar. It will look like you are a partier or a player. Don't use a photo with an ex-girlfriend; this will just make you look ridiculous. Don't be shirtless or wear a muscle shirt; it will look like you are a Guido or like you are full of yourself. You should be smiling in at least one of the photos, so that you look approachable. Most women don't respond to ads, since they have a lot of e-mail to deal with. Don't include your salary; it's no one's business, unless you want to meet a shallow materialistic bitch. Write a few things to describe what you like to do, such as hobbies, and what you are looking for. Don't be negative; keep it light. Below are samples of a do and a don't.

Do

> Hi, I'm a 35-year-old single male. I am in finance, 6'3", fit. I don't smoke, hardly drink. I enjoy spending quality time with my family and friends, quaint B&B's, sports, long hikes, and much more. I am seeking someone special, who is sweet, caring, family oriented, 28–35.

Don't

> Single **again** and looking. I am an average looking guy, 6'3" and 35. I am looking for **long sensual kisses and baths**. I am not into head games. You must be **hot, size 4, age 18 to 25**.

If you are looking for a committed relationship leading to potential marriage, only respond to ads of women who you could visualize being the mother of your children. Don't write to bimbos, high-maintenance gold diggers, or men haters. Their ads should stand out. If their ads include any of the following phrases, then skip over them: no players, no games, looking for a generous man, I love fine dining and shopping at Bergdorf's, looking for a hot guy, looking for someone to take care of me, used to the finer things in life, I'm spoiled, I'm open-minded, I'm sexy.

If you do write to ads that mention the phrases above, you'll find it to be a total waste of time. These women are out only for themselves and usually have no capacity to be giving or unconditional in a relationship. You will spend most of your time proving yourself and it will drain your bank account. If women write any of the following, beware because they may be very emotionally needy and more trouble than they are worth: connection, dream man, "in the clouds," intimacy, commitment, ex-boyfriend, ex-husband, "I've been hurt," "emotionally available," "in the stars," searching for the one, I recently broke up a long-term relationship, I believe in love at first sight. In most cases, if a woman brags too much about herself, then she is relying too much on her physical attributes: I am beautiful, I'm gorgeous, I have a great body.

Choose a woman who can define herself as caring, honest, sincere, cultured, well traveled, artistic, creative, thoughtful, and empathetic. A woman who has developed a personality beyond her looks is a much more suitable mate for a relationship, unless, of course, you want a selfish, self-centered bitch. Beware of a woman who is concerned with being up-to-date with the latest styles and obsessed with working out six days a week. You can tell what someone is obsessed with by how much the person talks about the topic. If someone talks about one topic over 20 percent of the time, then that topic is the person's obsession. For example, if the woman talks incessantly about her job, then she is very preoccupied with it. If the woman talks about diets constantly, then she is obsessed with dieting and her self-image.

HELPFUL HINTS

There are many ways to improve your personal ad. There is the obvious one of including good photos. The more subtle ones are the way that your ad is written. Simply changing a few words can make a great difference. I have listed some suggestions for elaborating on typical hobbies and interests as well as expanding on typical descriptive words that are commonly used.

Hobbies and Interests

Instead of This:	Write This:
Bike riding	Cycling through the Tuscan region
Boating	Sailing away on a catamaran, island hopping in the Caribbean via sailboat
Broadway shows	Theatre
Candlelight	Floating candles
Comedy shows	Cabaret
Dancing	Dancing barefoot in the sand to the sounds of the steel pan, dancing to the rhythm of the drums

Diving	Wreck diving 100 feet below, reef diving surrounded by a school of trumpet fish
Eating out	Exploring the gastronomy of exotic cuisine
Fresh flowers	Enjoying the rainbow of hues in tropical flowers, fresh cut sunflowers
Golf	Chasing a little white ball while enjoying everything nature has to offer
Horseback riding	Equestrian days through forest trails
Jogging	Feeling free as I run two miles by the shore
Lying on the beach	Soaking up rays as I feel the silky sand beneath my toes
Movies	Films/Foreign Films
Outdoor dining	Sharing a panini at a sidewalk café
Photography	Creating photographic art
Reading	Being taken away as I read every page of a *New York Times* bestseller
Skiing	Skiing in Vail at twilight, skiing down a black diamond in Vermont
Swimming	Swimming against the waves in ocean waters
Travel	Exotic travel to unique locales
Walking	Walking in fresh fallen snow
Working out	Feeling the rush after bench-pressing 200 pounds

Descriptive Words

Instead of This:	Write This:
Black	Noir, midnight
Blond	Flaxen, golden, honey
Blue	Sapphire, azure, lapis, cobalt
Brown	Chestnut, almond
Classy	Sophisticated
Down-to-earth	Earthy
Dreamer	Wanderlust
Fat, full-figured	Large, plus size, Rubenesque
Flirtatious	Charming
Funny	Comical
Gray	Salt and pepper
Green	Emerald, sea green, turquoise
Honest	Forthcoming, sincere
Housewife	Domestic goddess
Interested in ...	Passionate about ...
Interesting	Fascinating
Kind, likeable	Endearing
Kinky	Open-minded, adventurous
Love of life	Joie de vivre
Marriage-minded	Commitment-minded
Muscular, built	Buff
Not living at home	Independent
Positive thinking	Optimistic
Pretty, attractive, hot, beautiful	Graceful, outstanding
Red	Auburn, scarlet

Rich	Self-sufficient, self-made
Self-absorbed	Confident
Sensitive	Empathetic, perceptive
Short	Petite
Skinny	Thin, slim, fit
Smart, intelligent	Cerebral
Tall	Statuesque (for a woman)

Part IV
Just for Laughs

A Sampling of Responses

Subj: **GREAT LOVER**
Date: 11/19/2001 2:16:11 AM Eastern Standard Time
From: Daddy Warbucks
To: Follow Your Soul

Well, this is my last attempt at finding my soul mate if it's you. I will officially be on a long vacation from meeting and dating if we don't meet or click. About myself. I'm 42 never married no kids own my own house on the water, financially very secure, basically retired (not to brag but it's a fact) 6 ft 3 in 265lbs. I'm bald in the middle of my head but I make up for it in brains and soul. If this bothers you then stop reading. If not we will click for other reasons. I'm very giving, unselfish, know how to have a good time and know how to be with someone when they're sick. Been told I'm funny as well as a great lover. OK now what's your story?

Subj: **domination**
Date: 08/01/2001 3:59:57 AM Eastern Daylight Time
From: Houseslave9876
To: Follow Your Soul

i would like to introduce myself, i am a submissive looking to serve a dominant woman or a woman who has a dominant personality. i sincerely apologize if i have offended You. If this doesn't interest You, please just discard this e-mail and i will leave You alone. If i still have Your attention, thank You for continuing. i am an experienced and obedient, service oriented submissive who would like to serve as your personal servant. i have been trained in the art of serving superior women in a nonsexual service capacity. i do all manner of domestic chores: cleaning, dishes, laundry, ironing, kitchen, bathroom, etc. i will clean your house or apartment spotlessly with no strings attached. i am also a serious masochist who enjoys suffering for Your enjoyment.

i have various interests in domination and submission and would love to speak to you if you are interested. Thank You for taking the time to read this letter and i hope i have the opportunity and chance to correspond with you and talk of common interests. Although i am submissive, i am not a wimp and not lacking in being a man. If You have no interest in men but want to have one serve You, then let's talk, i would serve a lesbian or bisexual woman in any way You desire. If You are curious and want a man that would treat You like a queen, then let's talk. If i've piqued your curiosity, please respond. You won't be disappointed. Thanks!

Subj: **Marry Me?**
Date: 2/22/2003 7:46:24 PM Eastern Standard Time
From: ProposalPete
To: FollowYourSoul

Marry Me?

OK, maybe that is a bit much too soon but I wanted to give you an idea of how much I loved your profile. You look beautiful and sound even better.

I am active and athletic, love to travel, cook, and be with my family who I love very much. I could appreciate you in many ways.

Please take a look at my profile and if I sound like the kind of guy you'd like to meet, please write back (please send a copy to ProposalPete@marryme.com).

By the way, I am never sure how people react to my photo. I chose it because it says a lot about me. However, please bear in mind that I was on vacation and did not shave that day (some people thought I was a slop or had other odd comments).

Hope to hear back from you.
Ben

P.S. Regarding your photo...
WOWOWOWOWOWOWOWOWOWOWOWOWOWOWOWOWOWOWOWOWOW

Subj: **Yes—To Everything!!! (...politics aside)**
Date: 2/24/2003 4:16:00 PM Eastern Standard Time
From: The Yes Man
To: Follow Your Soul

Dearest Ms "InNY" (or may I call you simply, "Girl Next Door"?)

To answer your question, "Do you believe in magic?" I'd like to think that maybe it's just been borne upon me (no, I wouldn't say that to everyone...and no, I'm not being medicated).

Your narrative stands out like few others. Though my own listing is somewhat more flippant, I truly value every sentiment you expressed. You sincerely sound quite like the person I've waited so long to share the world with.

In essence, your profile seems familiar to me from some months back (or maybe it's just wishful thinking), but the photos and writings appear new and enhanced. After receiving notification and perusing your entry, I ran knocking at the doors adjacent to my apartment, then to the rest of the floor, then to the floors above and below me. The buildings next door were equally fruitless...I couldn't find you anywhere!

Could it be that I live in the wrong building? Is there a vacancy next to you, into which I might now move? Do I have time to pack?...Or am I the latest victim of some devilish hide-and-seek game on the part of an Internet enchantress?!! (...OK, so I'm easily fooled!)

As you can tell, I am experiencing an extraordinary degree of interest and optimism in you. If you abandon all sense of proper judgment in return, you'll be getting back to me shortly.

To looking forward!

The Yes Man

P.S.: I'll just assume that you already know you have the most gorgeous images on the 'net.

Subj: **SEXY**
Date: 10/20/2001 12:45:00 PM Eastern Daylight Time
From: Worth It
To: Follow Your Soul

U R VERY SEXY GET BACK 2 ME AND WE'LL CHAT U WILL LIKE WHAT U SEE

Subj: **great massage**
Date: 10/05/2001 7:29:58 AM Eastern Daylight Time
From: Bodybuilderbod
To: Follow Your Soul

hi saw your ad. you look very pretty. i am a 6 ft. 3 in. 220 lb. bodybuilderb—lond hair. i would like you to invite me over and cook me a nice steak. in return i will give you a great massage. i am the best massager. not for five minutes like those other guys i mean for hours. after we can spend the night together. you don't have to worry. all bodybuilders are safe. it's the little guys you have to watch out for. you can see my photo at my website. e-mail me if you are interested or you can call me at (800) 555-1212. Hercules

Subj: **Pen Pal**
Date: 5/3/02 10:04:34 PM Eastern Daylight Time
From: Linette
To: Follow Your Soul

Hi my name is Linnette i am looking for some one who would like to be a pen pal to a friend of mine. I know this is a weird request but he needs some friends to write to him. He is a 27-yr-old Hispanic male and is in jail. He got caught up in a mess when he was younger and now is paying for it. he's a great guy and is just looking for some-mail. If you would like to know anything else let me know and I will tell you what you want to know. Thank you!

Subj: **THE BEST**
Date: 09/22/2001 2:39:03 PM Eastern Daylight Time
From: Number One
To: Follow Your Soul

HELLO MY NAME IS ANDREW AND I LIKE YOUR PERSONAL. WRITE ME BACK IF YOU WANT TO GET TOGETHER.

Subj: **Paris**
Date: 4/22/2000 6:37:53 PM Eastern Daylight Time
From: Craig
To: Follow Your Soul

My company is sending me to Europe, including Paris, the first week in June and to Japan the third week in June. So I plan to stay in Paris and fly on to Tokyo instead of flying back to California for a week.

I have enough frequent flyer miles to take you too. NOT two or three of you, just ONE. Don't poutjust tell me why you are so much better than I could possibly deserve that you will make me forget every other woman I've ever met plus my own name if it weren't already embedded in my passport.

And I'll see if I can get reservations at the Tour d'Argent, one of the two Guide Michelin four star restaurants in all of France. I was there some years ago, before I learned the joys of wine. I ordered *la specialite de la maison, le canard presse* [pressed duck]. "And what would you like to drink with your meal?", asked the Parisian waiter (in English, since my French was not pure enough for him). "Why, I'll have a glass of milk", I replied. (As I said, I had not yet discovered the wonders of wine and I'd been raised pretty strictly.) "Sir", he responded very formally, "I cannot serve you a glass of milk." "Why not?", I asked in astonishment. "Because sir, the duck would not like it!"

I want to go back, order *"le canard presse"* again, along with a bottle of Chateau Neuf du Pape, '78.

Wanna come with me?

Craig

In Closing

I am sure after reading some of these stories that you might have said to yourself, "She must have been crazy to continue dating on the Internet!" I actually questioned my own sanity from time to time throughout those six years of my life.

I think people truly don't live their lives to the fullest if they always look at life rationally. Although almost all of these dates went wrong for one strange reason or another, and there were many other dates I went on that were quite ordinary, quite boring, and brought no connection with the other person.

Of course, those stories wouldn't be an interesting read. But I am glad that I did not give up on Internet dating, or else I would never have met my husband and be where I am today.

I have always led my life with a quote that I coined when I was just a girl: "Follow your soul." It is the soul that is your inner voice—the voice that speaks the truth.

I have learned that the present is a gift and should be cherished. Up until recently, I ignored the present and only hoped for the future.

Although I express time and time again in this book the desire to find a life partner, I want to make it clear it was *not* a need. A soul mate doesn't complete you; he enhances you. Some people enjoy their solitude. It is perfectly acceptable to be by one's self.

Finally, be true to yourself. The minute you start changing for another, you will realize that that person is not for you. The right person will love you exactly the way you are and have it no other way!

978-0-595-39115-8
0-595-39115-X

Made in the USA
Lexington, KY
09 February 2011